Text by **Paul Ardenne**

Graphic design by
Sylvain Enguehard

Ante Prima, Paris

Birkhäuser - Publishers for Architecture
Basel • Boston • Berlin

D1451224

à
Marc

Contents

LE FELLINI
FOUR-SCREEN CINÉMA

Location: Villefontaine - France
Commission: 1992 / Handover: 1994
Client: Villefontaine town council
Project manager: Franck Collet
Surface area: 1,500 m²
Cost: €1.5 million, incl. tax

Marc
Blaising

1992

B
METRO STATIONS
FOR THE VAL LINE
(RENNES)

C
PERFORMANCE HALL
(ORANGE)

FOOTBRIDGE

Location: Parc des Hauteurs – Lyon – France
Competition: 1992 / Handover: 1993
Client: Lyon City Council
Project manager: Philippe Leplaideur
Engineer: Marc Malinowsky
Length: 72m – width: 4m
Cost: €0.4 million, incl. tax

Ulrich
Kather

Philip
Murphy

CITÉ DE L'OR
(SAINT-AMAND-MONTROND)

AUTOMOBILE HUB
(BOURGOIN-JALLIEU)

Christophe
Michel

RESTRUCTURING
OF A HOSPITAL UNIT
(NANVILLE-LES-ROCHES)

BIOLOGY FACULTY BUILDING
(ORLÉANS)

PLACE HOCHE
AND UNDERGROUND CAR PARK
(RENNES)

LAURENT-MOURGUET SCHOOL

Location: Ecully – France
Competition: 1993 / Handover: 1997
Client: Rhône regional council
Project team: Franck Collet, Philippe Leplaideur,
Philippe Després
Surface area: 8,400 m²
Cost: €7.7 million, incl. tax

1993

SECONDARY SCHOOL
(TOUR-DU-PIN)

RESTRUCTURING-EXTENSION
OF A UNIVERSITY BUILDING
(VILLEURBANNE)

EXTENSION OF A REGIONAL
ARCHIVE BUILDING
(AIX-EN-PROVENCE)

REDEVELOPMENT
OF THE GRANDE-CÔTE GARDENS
(LYON)

UNIVERSITY BUILDING
(ALENÇON)

Franck
Collet

Élisabeth
Perrot

Marine
Bourron

Philippe
Després

Frédéric
Agnésa

Philippe
Leplaideur

Nathalie
Guerrin

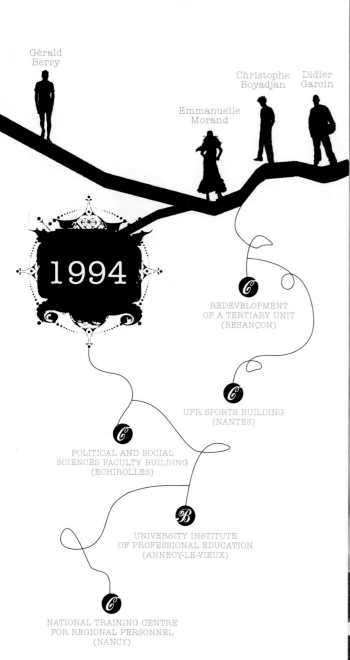

Gérald
Berry

Christophe
Boyadjan

Didier
Garcin

Emmanuelle
Morand

1994

REDEVELOPMENT
OF A TERTIARY UNIT
(BESANÇON)

UFR SPORTS BUILDING
(NANTES)

POLITICAL AND SOCIAL
SCIENCES FACULTY BUILDING
(ECHIROLLES)

UNIVERSITY INSTITUTE
OF PROFESSIONAL EDUCATION
(ANNECY-LE-VIEUX)

NATIONAL TRAINING CENTRE
FOR REGIONAL PERSONNEL
(NANCY)

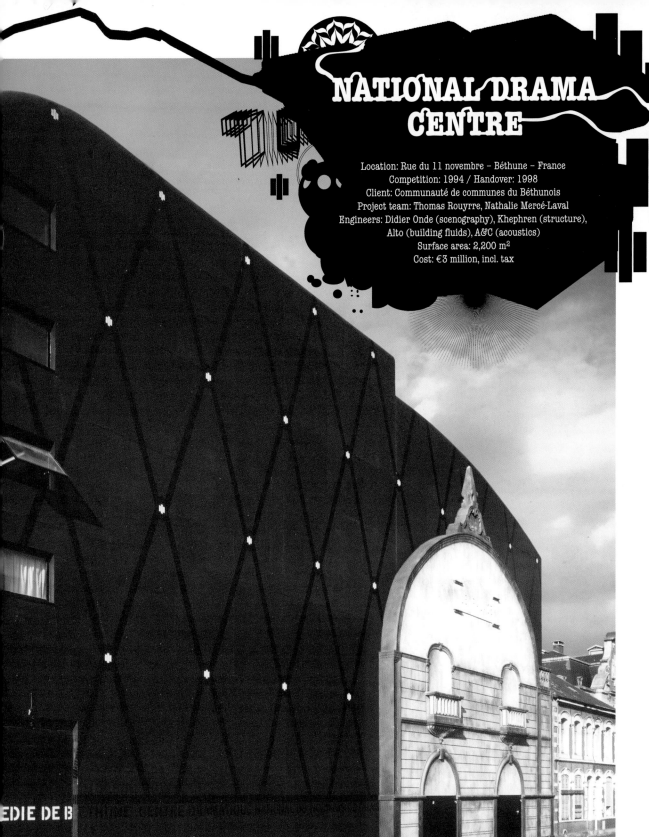

NATIONAL DRAMA CENTRE

Location: Rue du 11 novembre – Béthune – France
Competition: 1994 / Handover: 1998
Client: Communauté de communes du Béthunois
Project team: Thomas Rouyrre, Nathalie Mercé-Laval
Engineers: Didier Onde (scenography), Khephren (structure),
Alto (building fluids), A&C (acoustics)
Surface area: 2,200 m²
Cost: €3 million, incl. tax

AIRPORT
WAREHOUSE

Location: Nantes Airport – Bouguenais – France
Competition: 1994 / Handover: 1996
Client: Nantes Chamber of Commerce
Engineers: Nicolas Green (structure), OTH Ouest (building fluids)
Surface area: 5,100 m²
Cost: €2.6 million, incl. tax

Pascal
Desplanque

NATIONAL TRAINING CENTRE
FOR REGIONAL PERSONNEL
(PANTIN)

DESIGN SCHOOL
(NANTES)

REDEVELOPMENT
OF THE TOWN CENTRE
OF L'HAYE-LES-ROSES

SCHOOL
(SAINT-DENIS)

CULTURAL CENTRE
(BRUZ)

Valérie
Véron-Durand

Nathalie   Gerhard
Mercé-Laval   Kalohfer

Nicolas
Zucco

1995

TOLL PLAZAS
ON THE A16 MOTORWAY

Location: Abbeville Nord, Côte-Picarde, Le Touquet, Neufchâtel, Boulogne Sud (France).
Competition: 1995 / Handover: 1998
Client: Société des Autoroutes du Nord et de l'Est de la France
Project team: Jean-Francois Authier (project manager),
Sébastien Duron, Franck Collet
Engineers: Nicolas Green (structure and glass), Technip TPS
Surface area: 3,000 m²
Cost: €8 million, incl. tax

130

Anne
Traband

Thomas
Rouyrre

Jean-François
Authier

UNIVERSITY INSTITUTE
OF
INFORMATION TECHNOLOGY
AND LOGISTICS

1996

Location: University of Melun-Sénart– Lieusaint – France
Competition: 1996 / Handover: 1999
Client: Ile-de-France regional council
Project team: Sébastien Duron, Erik Kittler, Jean-Malo Pellet
Engineer: Séchaud-Bossuyt
Surface area: 2,200 m²
Cost: €3 million, incl. tax

Flavia
Nasio

Sébastien
Duron

C
OVERHEAD COVERING
FOR THE A1 MOTORWAY
(SAINT-DENIS)

B
INTERIOR REDEVELOPMENT
OF THE ADMINISTRATIVE PREMISES
OF THE POMPIDOU CENTRE
(PARIS)

Vincent
Jeune

Antony
Roubaud

NANTES AIRPORT CATERING BUILDING

Location: Nantes Airport – Bouguenais – France
Commisison: 1997 / Handover: 1998
Client: Actair
Project team: Jean-François Authier (project manager),
François Noir, Céline Parmentier
Engineers: Arcora (structure), Alto (building fluids),
ATPI (road network)
Surface area: 1,200 m²
Cost: €2 million, incl. tax

1997

Shirin
Raissi

Antoine
Barret

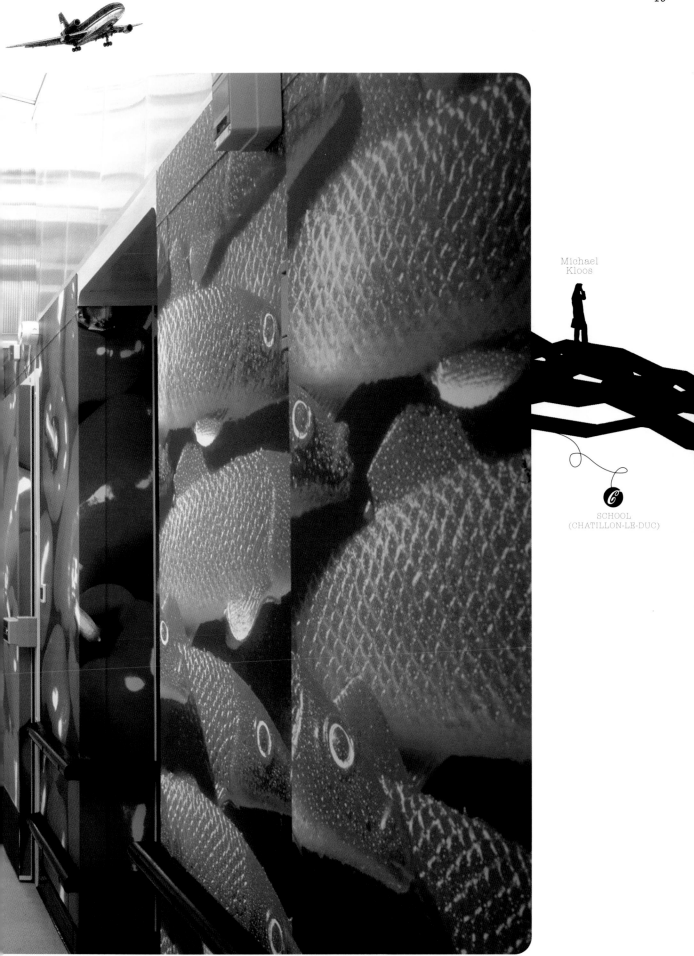

Michael
Kloos

𝒞

SCHOOL
(CHATILLON-LE-DUC)

Marc
Maes

Franck
Dutruel

LA COUPÔLE
CULTURAL CENTRE
(THEATRE AND CINEMA)

Location: Rue Théo Bachmann – Saint-Louis – France
Competition: 1997 / Handover: 2001
Client: Saint-Louis town council
Project team: Jalil Amor (project manager),
Marc Maes, Nicolas Zucco, Anne Feldmann
Engineers: AIC70 (structure), Alto (building fluids),
Peutz (acoustics), Cholley (economist)
Surface area: 4,500 m²
Cost: €10 million, incl. tax

INSTITUTE OF COGNITIVE SCIENCES
FOR THE CNRS – THE FRENCH
SCIENCE AND ENGINEERING
RESEARCH COUNCIL (BRON)

SOCIAL SCIENCES AND GEOGRAPHY
FACULTY BUILDING
(GRENOBLE)

Éric
Kittler

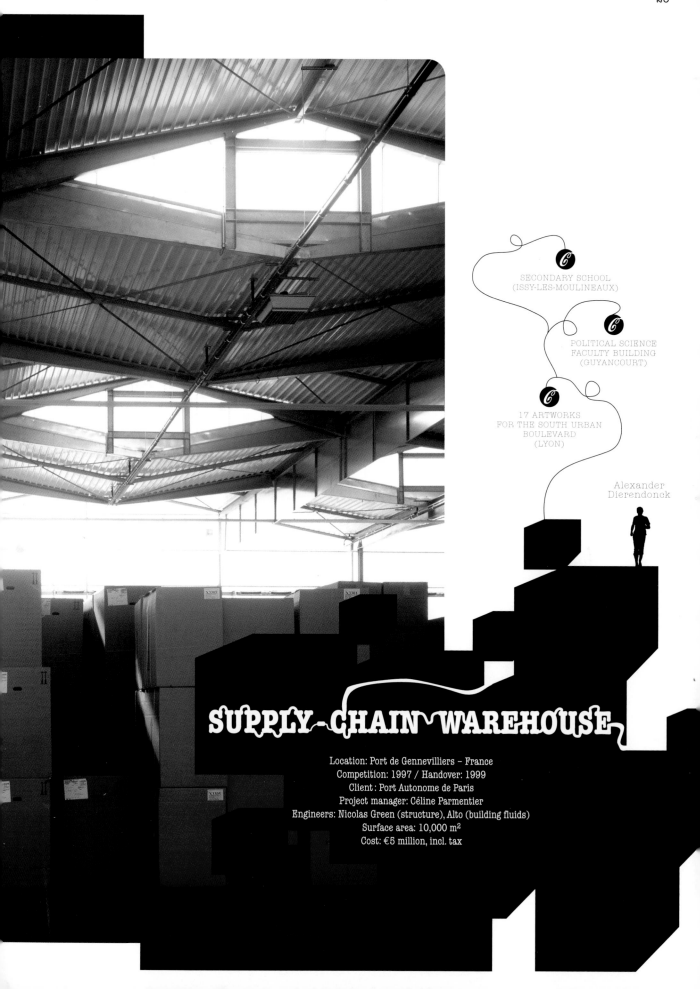

SECONDARY SCHOOL
(ISSY-LES-MOULINEAUX)

POLITICAL SCIENCE
FACULTY BUILDING
(GUYANCOURT)

17 ARTWORKS
FOR THE SOUTH URBAN
BOULEVARD
(LYON)

Alexander
Dierendonck

SUPPLY-CHAIN WAREHOUSE

Location: Port de Gennevilliers – France
Competition: 1997 / Handover: 1999
Client : Port Autonome de Paris
Project manager: Céline Parmentier
Engineers: Nicolas Green (structure), Alto (building fluids)
Surface area: 10,000 m²
Cost: €5 million, incl. tax

"Architecture makes for exchanges,
it is the space in which all sorts
of communications and encounters
are possible."

Manuelle Gautrand
"Re-thinking the city", DD, *Design Document
Series-06* (Seoul, February 2004), 9.

Paul Ardenne

Manuelle Gautrand or generous architecture

Unless otherwise indicated, all quotations from the architect in this essay are taken from an interview with the author.

The gist of an architectural approach is never more readily visible than when an architect is being playful and not taking herself too seriously. Take, for instance, **Bulle Bulle Casa** (2003), a temporary installation created by Manuelle Gautrand for the Tuileries Garden in Paris. The starting point was a competition organized by the French Institute of Architecture on the casual theme of "houses for animals", to be designed and eventually built for an exhibition. What Gautrand proposed for the occasion was a charming residential complex for gold fish:[1] columns composed of fish bowls filled with water, rising to different heights from their bases set directly in the Tuileries pond. Here were "high-rises", but made of giant transparent pearls glistening gracefully in the changing light of day and, in each bowl, there was the movement of the fish.

1
With the help of Marc Blaising and Hiroo Nishiyama.

But let's get down to the nitty-gritty of architecture. Born in 1961, Manuelle Gautrand obtained her degree in architecture in 1985 and opened an architectural practice with her associate Marc Blaising, first in Lyons and then in Paris. Straightaway, she developed a non-dogmatic style that quickly set her apart from established architects. Her early projects attracted notice by their sober refinement: a metallic footbridge in Lyon (1993) at the foot of Fourvière, delicately rising atop the massive piers of a former railway bridge; a multiplex cinema in Villefontaine (1994) with its airy entrance atrium and its play on colours and transparencies; a secondary school (Collège Laurent Mourguet, 1997) in Écully on the outskirts of Lyon, marked by the volume of its open spaces and its high overhanging roof which, mounted on slender pillars, is as aerial as it is protective. The buildings that Manuelle Gautrand constructed immediately thereafter –in particular, the National Drama Centre in Béthune, La Coupole Cultural Centre in Saint-Louis, and Airport Catering in Nantes– not to mention the numerous designs for competitions, evinced an even more personal and highly unconventional signature and put her on her way to the big league. The Gautrand style? Her buildings are all dissimilar yet they share an equal sense of function and context. To this she adds what soon established her reputation, namely, the pleasure factor, arising in her case from the joy that "architecturing" gives her. All of this is expressed in its own way by Bulle Bulle Casa: the efficiency, the adaptation to the surroundings, the keen sense of what is pleasing to the senses, and the search for originality.

"To please others and yourself" is what being an architect is all about, Manuelle Gautrand enjoys repeating. Architecture must be "emotional", even "violent", or it risks becoming simply uninteresting. Pragmatism, yes; imagination, yes too; sensualism, yes again.

Take, for instance, the **National Drama Centre in Bethune** (1998), an auditorium that Manuelle Gautrand had to anchor in a rough neighbourhood of a city in the Nord-Pas-de-Calais region of northern France. A scantily allotted floor space, a complicated ground plan, a few existing structures to be kept, and little in the way of material resources —at first glance, a true heartbreak. The architect defined the functional use of space (the main stage-related functions on the Boulevard Victor-Hugo side; the annex functions– the entrance, café, and upstairs offices – on the other), and then opted for big and rich. The building rises, first, and develops freely in space, exceeding the dimensions of the surrounding architecture. Its round, cambered envelope forms a shell in a reddish-brown varnished concrete, the colour of the local brick. The shiny surface is ornamented with a brick-like pattern of criss-crossing bands in the form of a Saint Andrew's cross; this abstract diamond pattern is not without recalling the large Xs solidifying the walls of local factories – a legacy from the industrial revolution. At each intersection of these mural lines, there is a delicate, dainty touch of phosphorescent white paint, with a jewel-like appearance. Together they compose a starry landscape, visible at night. Inside Manuelle Gautrand saturated the auditorium in red, the traditional colour of passion, in reference to classical theatres.

The key notion, then, in the case of the National Drama Centre in Bethune, is *investment.* The building does not spring out of nowhere; it draws substance from the context, picks up on local history and adds its own offer to it, on the order of extraction and federation. Where territory divides, Gautrand's architecture unifies, in a way that is at once familiar and novel. The architect here makes the most of a double inflection: on the one hand, the exacting analysis of the programme; on the other, the conception of a building that is specific but not arbitrarily tacked onto the original substratum.

Manuelle Gautrand was to give a highly significant nearly didactic illustration of this notion of "investment" in her *Éclaireuses* cultural platform project for Archilab 2002. The starting point was a disused warehouse on the banks of the Seine, a 200-metre-long parallelepiped. How could the "present" be injected back into this huge empty space? Manuelle Gautrand designed a mobile multi-purpose unit in the form of a shelter, the so-called *"Éclaireuse,"* reproduced a good many copies of the unit, and installed them all over the premises: on the roof of the building to turn it into a terrace, and in many spots inside the warehouse to generate places for meeting, playing, and creating. In addition, she adorned the existing structure with a superstructure that calls to mind an unwinding ribbon or band, with the new material running down and congealing there parasitically, for the purpose of revitalising the site (significantly, the prevailing colour is a flashy, attractive yellow). Alice Laguarda has aptly observed that the driving scheme of the *Éclaireuses* is the invasion or the graft of substances, as if the wider universe of the city encompassing the original building was conceived as a dual whole, made of permanent bodies, on the one hand, and nomad, if not mutant, corpuscles, on the other. "The figures of invasion and colonisation mark the Éclaireuses project," Laguarda writes, "The new construction 'embarks upon the conquest' of a drab, empty building [...]. Slowly but surely the invasion moves in from the side and from above until it has breathed 'new' life into it."[2] In sum, the "molecular" (micro, dynamic, rhizomatic) in support of the "molar" (macro, heavy, rooted), to use Deleuzian categories.

2
Alice Laguarda,
"Désobéissance,"
Inaccoutumance, exhibition
catalogue (Paris: Galerie
d'architecture, June-July,
2003), p.3.

CONTROLLED SHOWMANSHIP

Presence, as it were. Architecture must attract attention but not in a way that is out of phase. Injecting substance instead of imposing a representation. Inseminating and fertilizing. Eschewing technocratic soulless architecture, devoid of spontaneity. Refusing tedium and uniformity. Letting architecture express itself. Making it into a good cancer, a metastasis of urban joy. And a poem, too, so that the repertory of the built environment can be reinterpreted in its light.

Poeticising architecture. This is the purpose of the strategy of the "unaccustomed", to borrow a term from poet Saint John Perse (whom the architect frequently quotes), that runs through Manuelle Gautrand's work, a decisive strategy characterised by discovery, exploration, and boldness. Thus, she surmounts the **toll plazas on the A16 motorway** (1998) between Boulogne-sur-Mer and the Somme Bay with a long glass canopy printed with pictures of flowers, landscapes, or seascapes in a sensorial evocation of the stained-glass windows of the great cathedrals of northern France. For the conversion of the **Halles aux Farines in Paris** into a university building (design competition, 2001), rather than opting for the usual timid approach to renovation (that confines changes to the interior), she covered the old building front with a tubular network of staircases suggestive of a tree branching out: wide at the bottom of the building (where movement is concentrated) and narrowing as the staircases climb up the building like ivy. **For Airport Catering in Nantes** (1998), where meals for airlines are prepared, Manuelle Gautrand divided the site into two distinct units. One is a sober building in blue polycarbonate: this is the "inert" section where the non-perishable goods are stored. The other is a concrete building that houses the facilities for the preparation and storage of fresh produce. It benefits from soft overhead lighting and purposely sports a decorated interior that spells out the reference to food through giant enticing photographs of fish, fruit, and vegetables in what amounts to an unabashed apology of gourmandise.

The problem with aestheticising –which is also its limit– is that it risks turning gratuitous, that is, pretty but hollow. How does Gautrand avoid "art for art's sake"? Firstly, by giving aesthetics a citational function. Secondly, by countering the Parnassian system and making sure that the showmanship is not merely enjoyable but enjoyable and logical at once. Enjoyment combined with awareness is precisely what she delivers in her powerfully subtle design for **Citroën's showroom on the Champs-Élysées in Paris** (handover scheduled for 2006). The first pitfall was the location itself. Acquired by André Citroën in the 1920s, and used for other purposes for a quarter of a century, the space is deep, narrow, and extremely vertical; in addition it is situated in an environment that has increasingly assumed the character of a museum. The second pitfall has to do with the downturn in the symbolic status of the automobile, which has become a subject of tension due to traffic congestion, accident mortality, and pollution. It being understood, of course, that it is the function of the architecture and decor to help curb the irritation of state authorities in this regard. The proliferation since 2000 of single-brand car museums, showrooms, and factories designed as showcases is proof thereof: the PSA design centre in Vélizy, Volkswagen's "glass" factory in Dresden, and the Mercedes and BMW museums now under construction are just a few examples of how appearance and packaging are used to recharge the automobile's image battery.

Manuelle Gautrand's project for the Citroën showroom on the Champs-Élysées is conceived from two points of view. The first brings the automobile's *pars mythologica* into focus – a mythology in which Citroën participated fully all throughout its history with its Yellow Cruise Central Asia expeditions, its DS and 2 CV models, its African rallies, and so on. The vehicles are displayed on six exhibition platforms mounted on a mast running up to the roof, more than 20 metres high; visitors are offered a highly theatrical visual path proceeding up lateral ramps from the ground floor to the top of the showroom. The second concentrates on the emblematic dimension via Citroën's double chevron trademark, which the architect repeats on the building front, the roof, and straight up the rear wall by way of a lattice structure in glass and steel. This repetition begins at the bottom of the building on the surface of the original Citroën building –a wide flat glass front– and unfolds with increasingly pronounced complexity as it ascends to the top of the facade and the roof, in the manner of an origami. Lionel Blaisse gives the following description of the structure: "A gigantic grid in steel tube deploys in a single thrust a curve generating the unique volume that unites the vertical facade with the surbased rear. An outer skin made of clear glass panels, in rectangular, triangular, and diamond shapes, covers the space with an eleven-metre-wide glazed band, folded like a Japanese tangram. Judiciously tinted red in spots, the tangled grid of panels on the façade creates a pattern of the company's emblematic chevrons."[3] Gautrand's version of the Citroën showroom skilfully articulates the two symbolic dimensions attached to the automobile: the automobile as phallic symbol (its power, speed, and ability to dominate space are foregrounded by the vehicles presented on the platforms), and the automobile as womb (the cocoon, the comfort, and the shelter are suggested by the facade which curves out over the avenue as if it were gravid with what it is protecting from the exterior). The whole is packaged and decked out in a way that revives the ornamental vocation of architecture scorned by the moderns and draws it in the direction of art. As Lionel Blaisse rightly remarks again, we have here "a sensorial site of culture that communicates the essence of the brand in a single room which, instead of occupying a window display, invests the entire 25 metres of the [building's] height with an automobile sculpture-showcase."

3
Lionel Blaisse,
"La Spirale en mouvement de Manuelle Gautrand",
in *Archicréé* 305 (2002), p.90.

EFFICIENT GRACE

As we can see, there is nothing here of a specious subscription to the kind of exterior showmanship that has become so fashionable since the 1990s – the triumph, all too often, of the empty facade.[4] Gautrand's architecture is thoughtful. It gives itself and it has plenty to give, provided that there is coherence. The extension that Manuelle Gautrand designed for the **Modern Art Museum** in Villeneuve d'Ascq (handcover scheduled for 2007) demonstrates in every possible way this ongoing refusal of outrageous outbursts or megalomania. The formula proposed may well be of unmitigated originality (and this is the case for the five "arms" that Gautrand has butted against one end of the original construction by Roland Simounet and which seem to twist and crawl on the ground), the architectural statement remains nonetheless logical or, less neatly put, *adapted*.

What is exemplary about Manuelle Gautrand's project at Villeneuve d'Ascq is that it is simultaneously at odds and in tune with the main building. Gautrand's conception of the extension to the museum? Not a replication but a continuation, and an apparently polemical continuation, so different is the new

4
On this subject,
see the series of articles by Jean Vermeil,
Lionel Blaisse, and
Anne-Laure Egg
in "Façades spectacle en Europe et ailleurs",
Archicréé n°311
(November-December 2003), p.50-77.

from the old. At first glance, the sequence that the architect adds looks completely, almost provocatively, out of plumb with the work of her predecessor. Is the ingenious neo-modern Simounet's building a regular, repetitive, structured, linear, and hierarchical construction that keeps the sensorial at a distance? Then Gautrand apparently turns the tables on this initial scheme. Note the irregular seriality of the five "arm" graft that she operates on the initial body of the museum, the "hair locks" plan of the new constructed unit, the way that its tips fall onto the adjacent park, in a statement that is not far from expressionism, while the museum assumes an increasingly irregular appearance. Sheer madness? At closer scrutiny, there is not an iota of fury or hysteria in Manuelle Gautrand's addition. Consider the purpose of the extension, which is to house the Aracine collection of Art Brut, formerly located in Neuilly-sur-Marne. In the first place, this so-called "raw" art by autodidacts and madmen (codified in the 20th century first by Hans Prinzhorn and then by Jean Dubuffet) is replete with the selfsame twisted shapes that Gautrand, in the name of symbolic correspondence, encodes in her architecture. In the second, these works are fragile and cannot bear too much sunlight. For this reason, Gautrand tactically distributes a network of openings, with numerous small windows in the exhibition rooms to reduce daylight and a carefully calculated number of big windows, where possible, to provide generous views of the park. In addition, the "arms" that Manuelle Gautrand adds to the original building lean on it by picking up on its dimensions: inside the building museum-goers pass from the old areas to the new without experiencing the slightest change in scale. Finally there is nothing, not even the twisted shape of the arms, that does not owe something to the topography of the land. No violence is exerted upon the site; the forms simply follow the curves in the surface of the park.

A WELL-HELD POSITION

Let's imagine a time –still to come– when architecture will be integral with humankind. Not plainly humanist, on our scale, and quite simply adapted to our needs. Nor plainly spectacular, out of scale, and humiliating, exciting us, as an eye-catching figure would, with a dubious thrill. "Integral"? What I mean by that is an architecture that we would not experience as a banality, a punishment, or a treat but rather, on a day-to-day basis, as the chance given to our representations to be embodied in a built environment that singularises them. A prodigious architecture of building that would speak to us about us and that would integrate a great deal of our complexity combined with our desire to draw pleasure from the real, on a Dionysian mode, but that would also grant us a comfortable, reasonable place, this time on an Apollinarian mode. An architecture moving between rationality and transcendence, between wisdom and disorder, between submission and excess – exactly like we do.

The Gautrand method consciously integrates equal portions of order and disorder. It is determined to be useful (architecture and art, she says "should not be confused"), but also inventive, receptive to alterity and to the option of the singular offer. Creation, not reproduction. "The standard models that have been mechanically reproduced for the past fifty years are totally outdated and need to be rethought," observes Manuelle Gautrand,[5] emphasising the need for places "where people can meet, inventive places that encourage community living."[6] Architecture must not in any way aggravate isolation or individualism; on the contrary, it must promote the sensorial fusion and wellbeing of the user.

5
"Réflexions sur la Haute Qualité Environnementale", in Marc Émery, *Innovations durables – Une autre architecture française* (Ante Prima/Birkhäuser, Paris, Basel, Boston, Berlin, 2002), p.86

6
DD, Design Document Series, op. cit., p.10.

The architect's quest for re-humanisation is most convincingly exemplified by her project for the **Pinault Foundation of Contemporary Art** (competition, 2001) to be located right at the heart of the premises of Renault's former Boulogne-Billancourt factory, shut down in the early 1990s. The museum site is situated at the end of Île Seguin where the island comes to a point and is surrounded by the river Seine and isolated from the inaccessible neighbouring banks of Sèvres and Meudon. Straightaway, Gautrand designed a triangular building whose tip, instead of marrying the tip of the island, is pointed in the opposite direction, toward the centre. The option taken –reversing the generating lines of the original site– is that of fanning out. Instead of projecting the user into a narrowing space, the visit of the building and the progression into its depth correspond to an outward movement of spatial expansion. The very structure of the building heightens this fanning out. The floors are not exactly superposed; they are positioned like segments of an unfolding fan and provided with inviting patios offering panoramic views. Footbridges are thrown over the river, connecting the building directly to the banks in a way that anchors it in its surroundings while facilitating pedestrian traffic. In the same vein, the contact with the water is omnipresent (suspended walkways and a floating restaurant designed in a flexible material), as is the contact with the sky (glass ceilings curving in towards the centre of the exhibition rooms, in the manner of suspended bosses in Plantagenet or flamboyant Gothic style architecture). Beyond this very cosy, basically amniotic, layout, the fascination expected from architecture is by no means neglected. The entire building is sheathed in a tinted glass envelope-skin. It reflects the surroundings –the sky, the water, and the city– during the day and creates a kind of Chinese lantern effect at night.

The method applied by Manuelle Gautrand to the Pinault Foundation project clearly evidences the different ingredients of her *organon.* As we have seen, each one of her projects is invariably organised as a function of a contextual given. Thus for the Béthune Drama Centre, discussed above, two existing structures were preserved: a house and a 1930s cinema front. For Rambouillet, where the artist was in charge of designing a vast arts complex for creation and performances, with housing for resident artists (*Centre de creation et de diffusion de spectacles*, handover scheduled for 2007), Gautrand opted to place the buildings in line with the very straight alignment of existing building fronts on the street. Each of the four buildings is disconnected from its neighbours: this echoes the spatial structuration of the site, with its detached houses ("Architecture," Gautrand insists, "is also solids and voids"). Lastly, the large glass panels illustrated with photographic prints over the toll booths on the A16 motorway do not have a uniformly decorative function. Citing the environment in which they are located and its traditional crops –the *ager*, brutalised and irreversibly altered by the motorway's broad path– they serve as a metaphorical recreation of the unity of the landscape (in much the same way as "animal paths" installed along motorways serve as concrete recreations of this unity for the wildlife).

The second aspect of the Gautrand method is narrative. Each of her projects undertakes to modulate its own relationship to the setting and to local traditions in narrative terms. The "story"–of the *locus,* of what gestures here or there in it, its history, its transformations, and so on– acts as a focus of humanisation and a way of refusing the legendary autism of modernism that has no "history" to write of the building other than that of the promoter's authoritarian thinking. For Gautrand, a construction is never an isolated statement. It speaks, communicates, and irradiates: "Architecture tells stories, sustains and stimulates imagination, encourages us to share."[7]

7
Ibid., p.9.

ARCHITECTURE AS PATCHWORK

No disconnection. Architecture, unless it is being deliberately irrespons-ible, is an art of constraints. Disregarding them is risky business (and leads to overspending, non-suitability for users, functional misuse, disaffection, etc.). Are we facing a housing crisis, a time when issues of energy conservation and the environment are of major concern? For **Solaris** (handover scheduled for 2006), a complex of 100 housing units in Rennes, Manuelle Gautrand goes well beyond the technocratic standards set by the HQE (High Quality Environment) directive. The design of the three linear "ecological" buildings with rounded corners is based on a thorough analysis of sun exposure, heat circulation, and the incorporation of landscape into architecture. The southern fronts are generously provided with openings. Each apartment has a suspended balcony, which serves as a solar heat collector in winter and as a buffer zone to keep out hot air in summer. In addition the apartments are conceived so as to allow air to circulate from the southern facade to the north of the building. Neither the choice of tree species nor their placement on the southern perimeter is left to chance: deciduous species screen out the sun in summer but let the daylight in unimpeded in winter. The result? Eco-architecture combined with a delightful quality of life, seldom found in collective housing projects. "The validity of a HQE project cannot be confined to its technical performances, its energy efficiency, or the overblown quantity of equipment generated," Manuelle Gautrand remarks. "The HQE is added value architecture and it necessarily involves a stylistic search [...] and, especially, an accord between the building and the setting. Architectural poetics always turns out to be compatible with new technologies."[8]

There are, then, all these buildings and an equal number of adventures. Gautrand's architecture is contingent, Darwinian, and interferential. Recent confirmation can be found, if need be, in her project for the **Gaîté-Lyrique** in Paris (handover scheduled for 2007), a neo-classical theatre, a "grotto", to use Gautrand's term, to be converted into a centre for contemporary music. The building is so thoroughly segmented that circulation is difficult. This time, it is a "digital ribbon" in resin, with electronic light-emitting indications all over, that spreads through the space and confers its identity to the architectural gesture. In addition, the nomad modules, "run in" during the *Éclaireuses* project, are put to concrete use in the Gaîté-Lyrique: some of these small units will house reception services, reading areas, or technical facilities, others will serve as cloakrooms or rehearsal spaces for musicians. In Manuelle Gautrand's work, there is no mechanical repetition of a model and no restatement of a genre that would constitute a "style", by its formal concentration. It is useless to look for an effect of reiteration in her architecture. What you will find instead is just the opposite: diversity and a continual reassessment. The result is an architectural patchwork.

8
Manuelle Gautrand, "Réflexions sur la Haute Qualité Environnemental", in Marc Émery, *Innovation durables – Une autre architecture française*, op. cit., p.86.

ECLECTICISM?

Manuelle Gautrand or the eschewal of a unifying principle. Some will maliciously claim that this boils down to eclecticism, understood, of course, in its worst sense, as non-choice and a readiness to accept anything. I beg to differ. Eclecticism would amount to using all means available, yielding to an asinine rehash, espousing the fluctuating mechanisms of seduction, and offering contracting authorities whatever it takes to flatter their expectations or egos.

9
In an interview with
François Chaslin on
the *Métropolitains* radio
programme, France
Culture, February 2003.

Manuelle Gautrand, need I recall, has lost quite a number of contests ("We spend our time losing them," she comments[9]), and not only because of the heated competition. Her choices betray an exigency that contradicts standardized, trendy architecture and so they can be quite simply disconcerting. This was the case recently with the **Casino** project in Saint-Étienne (competition, 2004), even though the building – (which Gautrand conceived as the outcome of an invasion of micro-office units trooping through one after another in single file to colonize the area) was indisputably a model of originality. Similarly, on occasion, Manuelle Gautrand has had to abandon a project already underway because her original concept could no longer be respected. It happened recently with an office-building project in Orléans (which had a unique, highly sculptural and suggestive plan in the shape of an arrow), after a disagreement with the property developer over the makeup of the facade glazing. This intransigence bespeaks a well-defined viewpoint and a personal engagement. Architecture is a functional discipline that brings together in practice a variety of actors and therefore it involves all sorts of negotiations, and these are clearly unavoidable. But up to a point. Past this point of no return, what were necessary discussions of problems related to a project's concrete construction end up debasing the architectural vision itself.

We know only too well that the cultural value and influence of an architect usually depend on criteria that have little to do with architecture. But cultural value can be seen, in fact, much less in fame or in success than in resonance. By this I mean a type of architecture that expresses its period, that knows how to convey a passion for its times, that has a concordant manner of inhabiting the world, neither autonomist nor cosmetic. Sustained by a democratic ideal of social ethics and collective responsibility, attached to questions of wellbeing, ecology, and the current urban crisis in the Western world, the architecture of Manuelle Gautrand is of this type: it is well and truly in "resonance" with the present, our common present. It is an architecture well aware of the traps of modernism (dehumanisation, abstract conception of building, technocracy, etc.), aware as well of the ravages of postmodernism and its moronic historicism, and aware finally of the vacuity of deconstructivism's formal games (If we are living in a shattered world, then let's make buildings that look when they are new as if they were already destroyed[10]). It is an architecture that stands with resolution at a respectable distance from heavy-handed statements as from metaphor-isations, be they retro or theatrical.

10
See Daniel Libeskind's
comments on his design
concept for the Imperial
War Museum in
Manchester based on
a shattered globe.
In *Construire le futur:
d'une enfance polonaise
à la Freedom Tower*,
Paris: Albin-Michel, 2005).

11
Cf. Jean-François Lyotard,
The Postmodern Condition
(Minneapolis: University
of Minnesota, 1978).

12
The question was raised
in regard to her extension
for the Modern Art Museum
in Villeneuve-d'Ascq.
Interview with François
Chaslin on Métropolitains,
op.cit.

IDEOLOGY-FREE AND GENEROSITY

Born in 1961, Manuelle Gautrand belongs to the post sixties generation that came of age in the 1980s, a period of doubt and decline in overarching systems of Western thought.[11] Hers is a generation more pragmatic and circumspect than disenchanted, one that has learnt to hold both tradition and utopia at bay. (Archigram had genius, no doubt, but perhaps not enough interest in wellbeing). No getting worked up; no granting credit to strategies of combat (architecture can be *gentle*) or to excesses of style (it must be *liveable* too). And especially, no ideology. Asked one day by journalist and historian François Chaslin about whether "joy" was part of her conceptual arsenal, Manuelle Gautrand made this telling response: "Yes, joy is an essential thing. Architecture must trigger emotion, it must be a source of surprise, gaiety, pleasure, and discovery."[12]

Gautrand enjoys repeating, and not without reason, that architecture is a reality "in between". Like transportation and public space, she adds. In day-to-day life, between the moment we leave our homes in the morning and the moment we come back to them at night, we come up against architecture wherever we turn, without the least hope of escape. Everywhere a "being-there" reigns supreme that we have no guarantee will suit us or will be to our liking and that most of the time we simply have to put up with. And who could deny that the moderns gave us shovelfuls of architecture to *endure*? Their incorrigible abstraction, their formalism, their concern with yield, with all sorts of yields (maximizing building costs, integration, regulation, and standardisation) will have generated a technocratic city of minimum urbanity. For the architect today, it is matter of working against this reality, even if it means disobeying; a matter, as Manuelle Gautrand says, of opposing oppressive cities, conceived as "functional machines" that "have nothing to recount". "Cities have to open up to experimentation in the same way as the arts and sciences," she writes. "Innovation always proceeds from disobedience, a certain refusal of established models."[13]

> This stand against domineering architecture, coming from an architect, is not a superficial posture. All the more so insofar as it is accompanied by a desire to promote a friendly "narrative", a familiarity, and a source of surprise, but one that is *acceptable*, related to local representations, expectations, or prospects. Such a conception overtly puts into its place the approach that is generally attached to proud architecture and wedded to concepts of power and authority. The intention is clear: to leave behind the imperative of Olympian personalization, ordinarily the cause of all those grand gestures that make for pretentious buildings. And prefer what to it? An architecture informed by virtue, context, respect, and pleasure, mindful that from its womb life emerges enhanced, including the life of the imagination. In substance, sheer generosity.

13
DD, Design Document Series-06, op. cit., p.9.

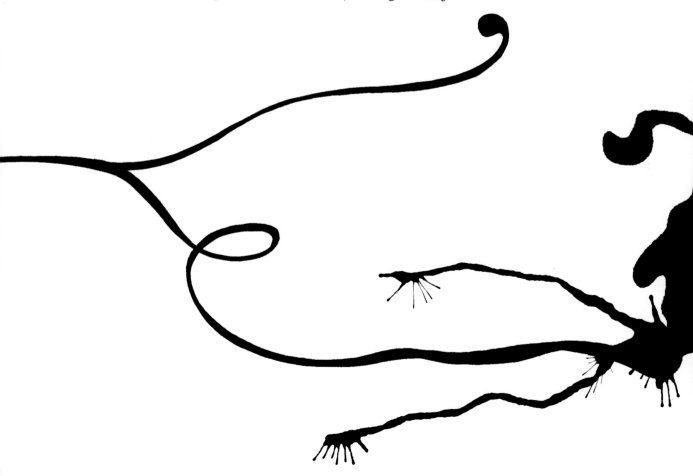

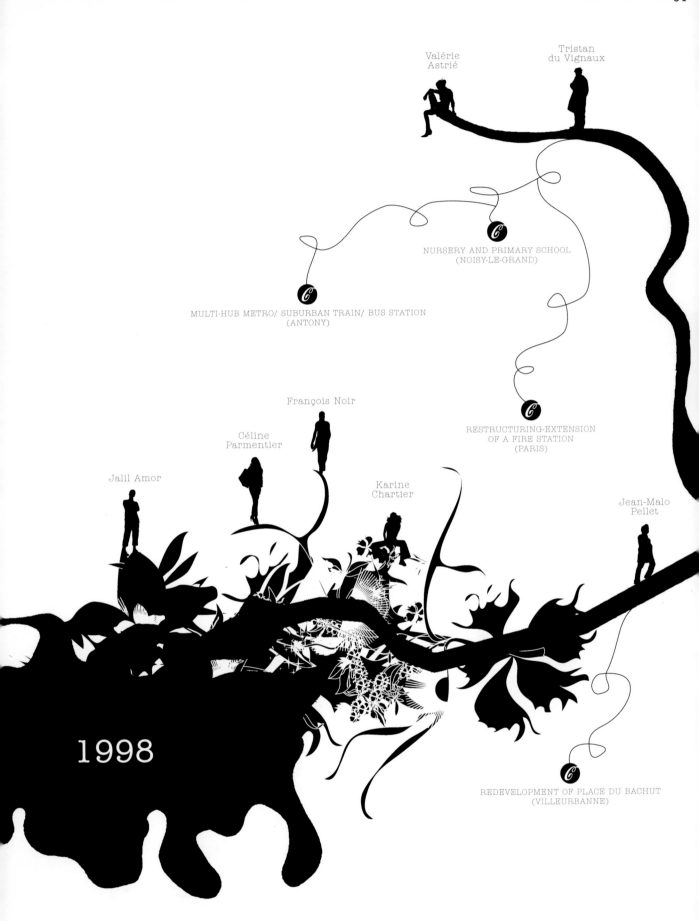

Valérie
Astrié

Tristan
du Vignaux

NURSERY AND PRIMARY SCHOOL
(NOISY-LE-GRAND)

MULTI-HUB METRO/ SUBURBAN TRAIN/ BUS STATION
(ANTONY)

François Noir

Céline
Parmentier

Jalil Amor

Karine
Chartier

RESTRUCTURING-EXTENSION
OF A FIRE STATION
(PARIS)

Jean-Malo
Pellet

1998

REDEVELOPMENT OF PLACE DU BACHUT
(VILLEURBANNE)

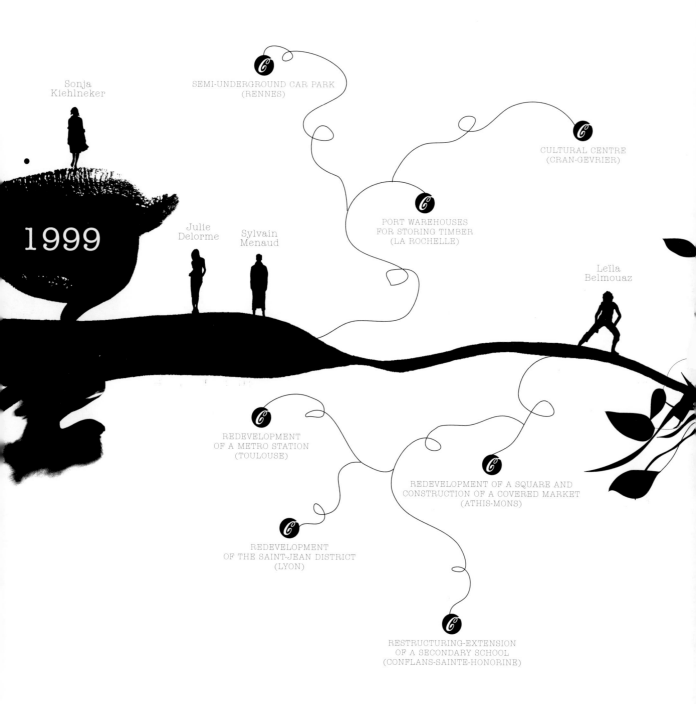

1999

Sonja
Kiehlneker

Julie
Delorme

Sylvain
Menaud

Leïla
Belmouaz

SEMI-UNDERGROUND CAR PARK
(RENNES)

CULTURAL CENTRE
(CRAN-GEVRIER)

PORT WAREHOUSES
FOR STORING TIMBER
(LA ROCHELLE)

REDEVELOPMENT
OF A METRO STATION
(TOULOUSE)

REDEVELOPMENT OF A SQUARE AND
CONSTRUCTION OF A COVERED MARKET
(ATHIS-MONS)

REDEVELOPMENT
OF THE SAINT-JEAN DISTRICT
(LYON)

RESTRUCTURING-EXTENSION
OF A SECONDARY SCHOOL
(CONFLANS-SAINTE-HONORINE)

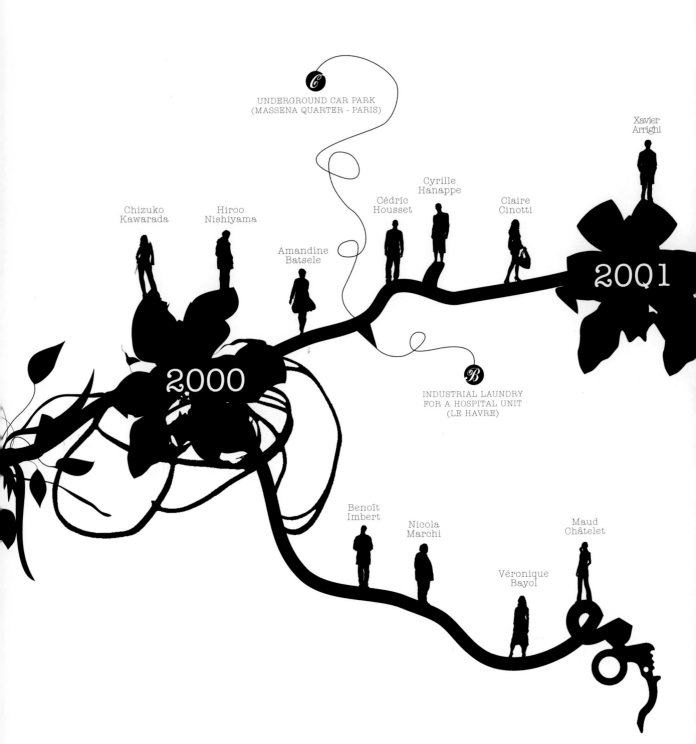

UNDERGROUND CAR PARK
(MASSENA QUARTER - PARIS)

Xavier
Arrighi

Chizuko
Kawarada

Hiroo
Nishiyama

Cyrille
Hanappe

Cédric
Housset

Claire
Cinotti

Amandine
Batsele

2001

2000

INDUSTRIAL LAUNDRY
FOR A HOSPITAL UNIT
(LE HAVRE)

Benoît
Imbert

Nicola
Marchi

Maud
Châtelet

Véronique
Bayol

Anne
Feldmann

Bertram
Brecht

B

"SOLARIS"

Residential complex and socio-cultural centre

The three wings

100 ecological apartments, a socio-cultural space wrapped in a smooth, water-green concrete shell and pierced with both hollow and jutting oriel windows. In winter, these windows heat the air like greenhouses, and in summer their glazing can be taken off to form spacious terraces.

Design concept and layout of the oriel windows (terrace-gardens)

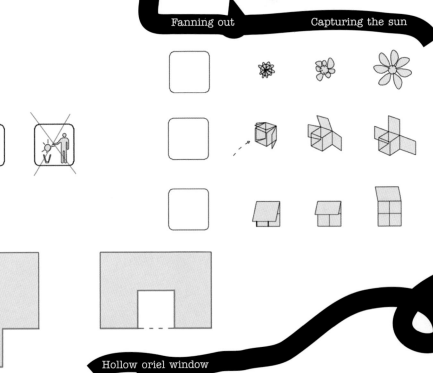

Fanning out   Capturing the sun

Jutting oriel window

Hollow oriel window

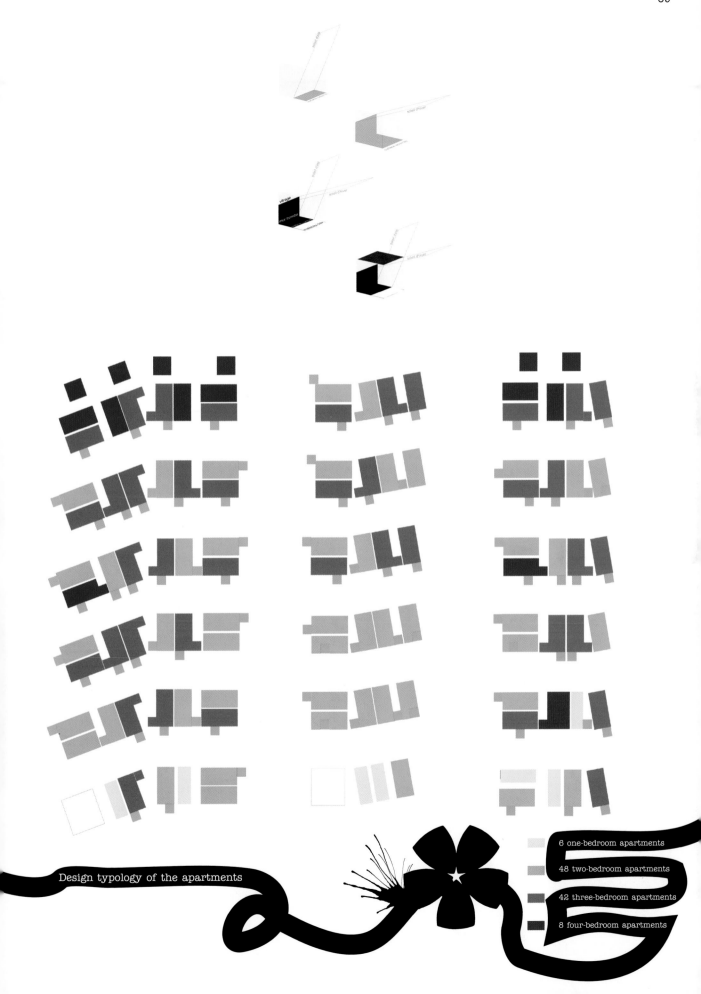

Design typology of the apartments

6 one-bedroom apartments

48 two-bedroom apartments

42 three-bedroom apartments

8 four-bedroom apartments

OFFICE BUILDING IN ORLÉANS

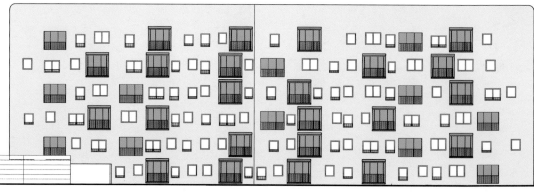

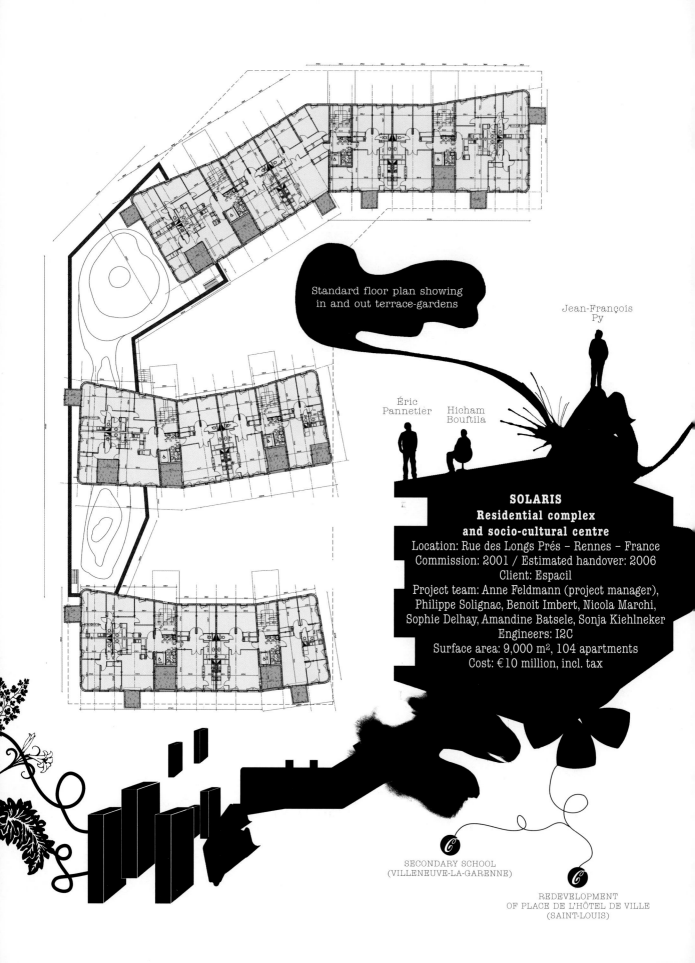

Standard floor plan showing
in and out terrace-gardens

Jean-François
Py

Éric
Pannetier

Hicham
Bouftila

SOLARIS
Residential complex
and socio-cultural centre
Location: Rue des Longs Prés – Rennes – France
Commission: 2001 / Estimated handover: 2006
Client: Espacil
Project team: Anne Feldmann (project manager),
Philippe Solignac, Benoit Imbert, Nicola Marchi,
Sophie Delhay, Amandine Batsele, Sonja Kiehlneker
Engineers: I2C
Surface area: 9,000 m², 104 apartments
Cost: €10 million, incl. tax

SECONDARY SCHOOL
(VILLENEUVE-LA-GARENNE)

REDEVELOPMENT
OF PLACE DE L'HÔTEL DE VILLE
(SAINT-LOUIS)

Hermann
Kohlhöffel

FRANÇOIS PINAULT FOUNDATION OF CONTEMPORARY ART

Four decks laid on the site transform the island's
natural curves and fan out in an open
and inviting design. Poised over the river Seine,
the structure is clothed in solid glass scales,
giving it a wet, glossy aspect, as if it had just
stepped out of the water.

Sophie
Delhay

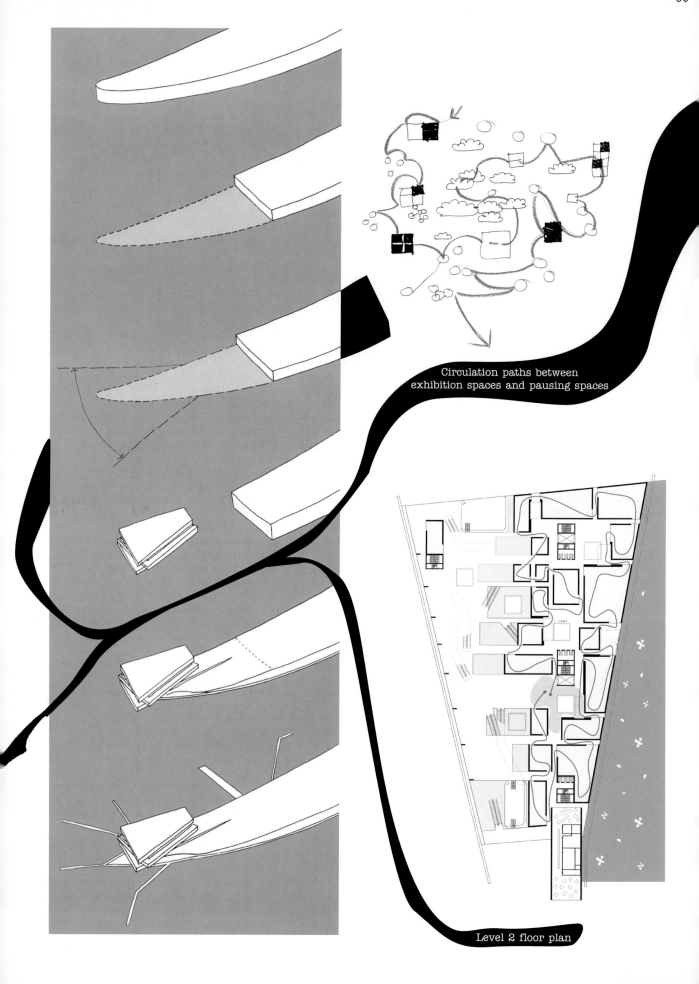

Circulation paths between
exhibition spaces and pausing spaces

Level 2 floor plan

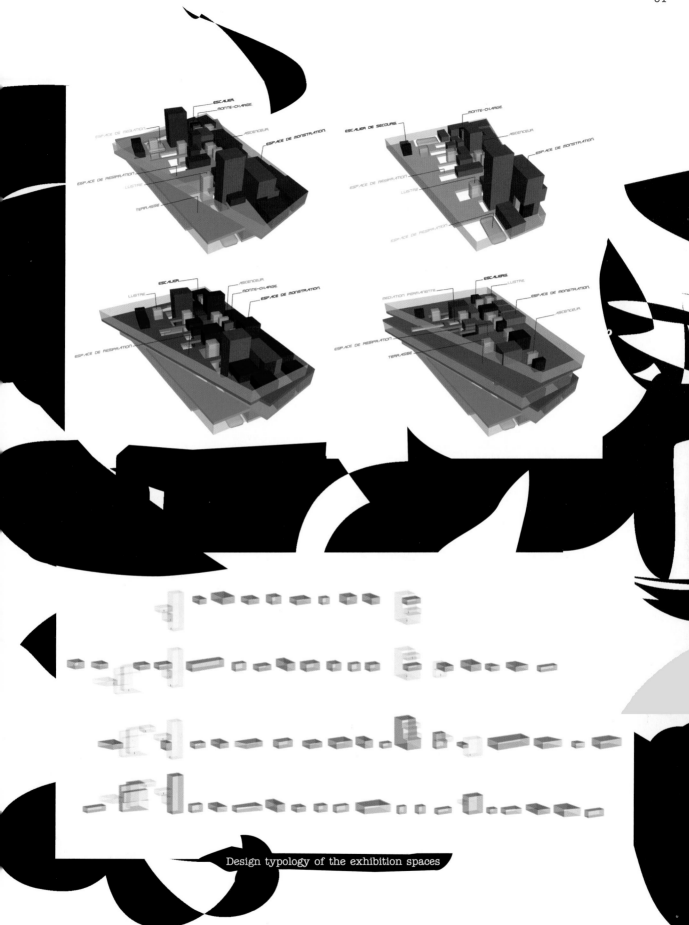

Design typology of the exhibition spaces

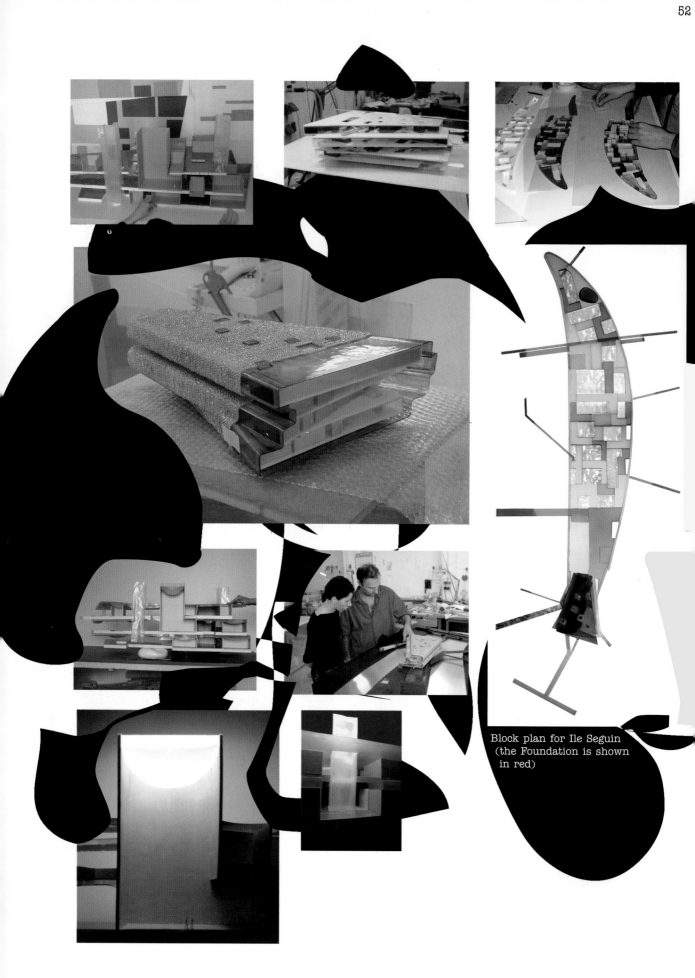

Block plan for Ile Seguin
(the Foundation is shown
in red)

The ceilings: a glass wave

Cross-sections

BULLE BULLE CASA
COLLECTIVE HOUSING
FOR GOLDFISH IN THE TUILERIES GARDENS, PARIS

FRANÇOIS PINAULT FOUNDATION OF CONTEMPORARY ART
Location: Île Seguin – Boulogne-Billancourt – France
Competition: 2001
Client: François Pinault - Artemis
Project team: Hermann Kohlhoffel, Eric Pannetier, Sophie Delhay,
Jean-François Py, Hiroo Nishiyama, Chizuko Kawarada
Engineers: Renaud Pierard (museum layout), R.F.R (structure),
Alto (building fluids), LTA (economist), Casso (safety)
Consultants: Paul Ardenne, Chrisophe Le Gac, Alice Laguarda
Surface area: 34,000 m²
Cost: €150 million, incl. tax

RESIDENTIAL COMPLEX
COMPRISING 260 APARTMENTS
(MONTÉVRAIN)

"La Halle aux Farines" UNIVERSITY BUILDING

Like a large wardrobe, the building is filled with classrooms and lecture theatres. It winds upwards and comprises meeting spaces that climb along the flank of the west facade, forming a huge composition of stairs shaped like fruit trees.

Sections of the circulation tube

Vertical circulations – an arborescence of tubes running along the façade

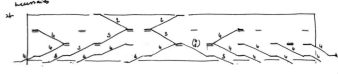

The circulation tubes envelope the former flour-exchange building

Cross-section showing classrooms and lecture theatre

R+5

R+4

R+3

R+2

R+1

RdC

Sandra
El Ammany

Benoît
Stehelin

La Halle aux Farines
UNIVERSITY BUILDING
Location: Left bank of the river Seine-Paris
(13th *arrondissement*) – France
Competition: 2001
Client: EPMOTC
Engineers: Khephren (structure),
Arcora (envelope), Alto (building fluids)
Surface area: 15,000 m²
Cost: €21 million, incl. tax

Classrooms

Offices

Student leisure area

University canteen

Yves
Tougard

CONTEMPORARY
MUSIC
AUDITORIUM

Miguel
Conde Silveira

Stéphane
Curtelin

Crystel
Cannone

Denis
Favret

Philippe
Solignac

**An incredible roof spans the performance area,
giving rise to a multicoloured, animated and at the same time baroque
space. Designed as a softy unfolding redesigned sky,
it covers a life of festivity.**

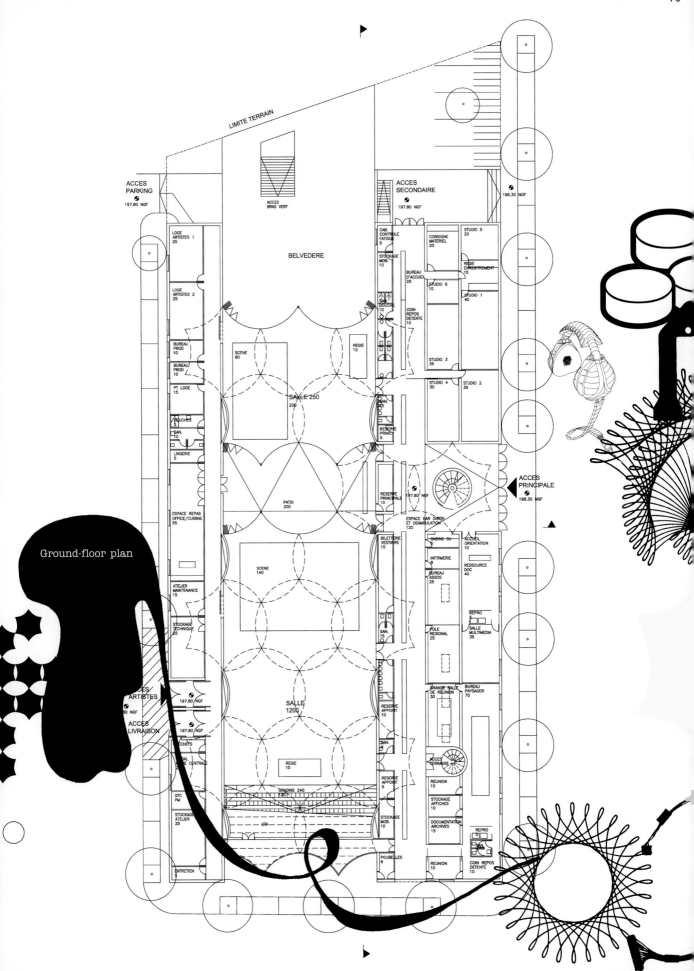

Ground-floor plan

LIMITE TERRAIN

ACCES PARKING
197.80 NGF

ACCES BRAS VERT
197.80 NGF

ACCES SECONDAIRE
197.80 NGF

198.30 NGF

BELVEDERE

LOGE ARTISTES 1 25

LOGE ARTISTES 2 25

BUREAU PROD 10

BUREAU/PROD 10

PT LOGE 15

DOUCHES 5

SAN. 10

LINGERIE 5

ESPACE REPAS OFFICE/CUISINE 55

ATELIER MAINTENANCE 15

STOCKAGE TECHNIQUE 25

ACCES ARTISTES
197.80 NGF

ACCES LIVRAISON
197.80 NGF

DECHETS

LOCAL TGBT CENTRALE

GTC PM

STOCKAGE ATELIER 25

ENTRETIEN 5

SCENE 90

SALLE 250 200

REGIE 10

PATIO 200

SCENE 140

SALLE 1200

REGIE 10

GRADINS 240 120

STOCKAGE MOB.

CTA

CAB. CONTROLE FATIGUE 5

STOCKAGE MOB. 10

BUREAU D'ACCUEIL 25

SAN. DOUCHE 10

COIN REPOS DETENTE 10

SAN.

RESERVE PRINC. 5

RESERVE PRINCIPALE 10

BILLETTERIE VESTIAIRE 15

SAN. 15

RESERVE APPOINT 10

SAN.

RESERVE APPOINT 5

STOCKAGE MOB. 10

POUBELLES 6

CONSIGNE MATERIEL 20

STUDIO 5 20

REGIE ENREGISTREMENT 15

STUDIO 6 10

STUDIO 1 40

STUDIO 3 35

STUDIO 4 30

STUDIO 2 35

197.80 NGF

ACCES PRINCIPALE
198.30 NGF

ESPACE BAR DISTRI ET DEAMBULATION 120

CABINE DJ 9

INFIRMERIE 8

BUREAU ASSOS 25

POLE REGIONAL 25

GRANDE SALLE DE REUNION 30

ACCES TERRASSE

REUNION 10

STOCKAGE AFFICHES 10

DOCUMENTATION ARCHIVES 15

REUNION 10

ACCUEIL ORIENTATION 10

RESSOURCE DOC 40

REPRO

SALLE MULTIMEDIA 35

BUREAU PAYSAGER 70

COIN REPOS DETENTE 10

REPRO 5

SAN.

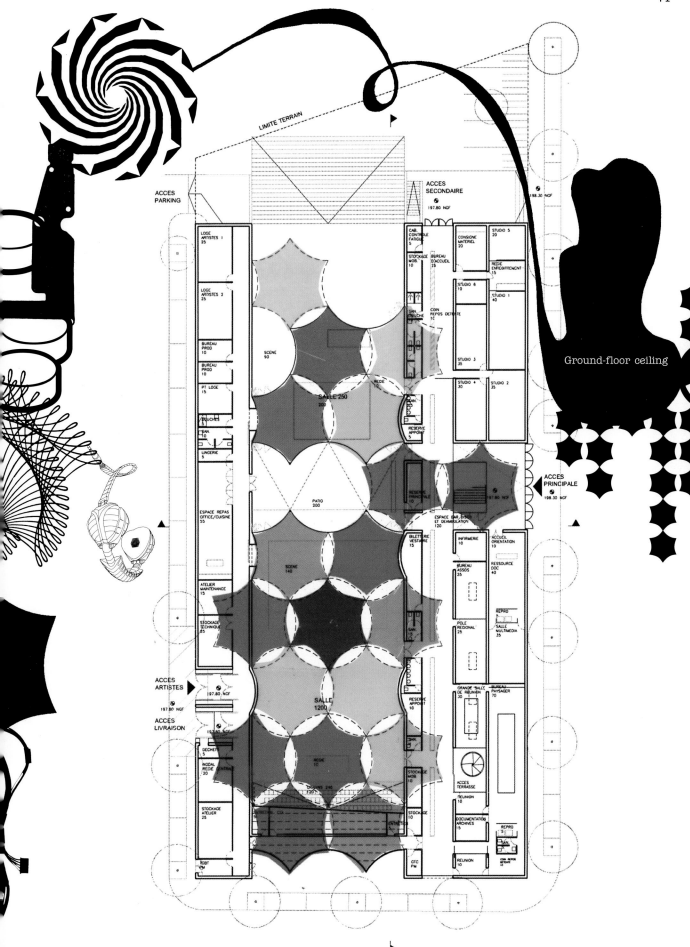

Ground-floor ceiling

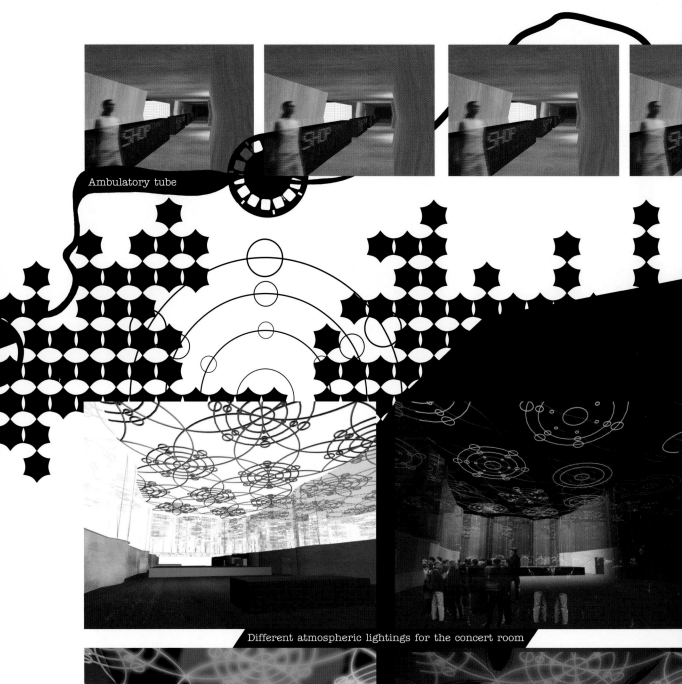

Ambulatory tube

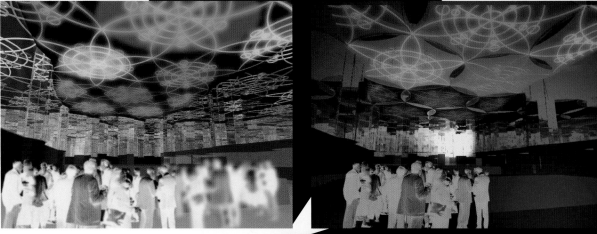

Different atmospheric lightings for the concert room

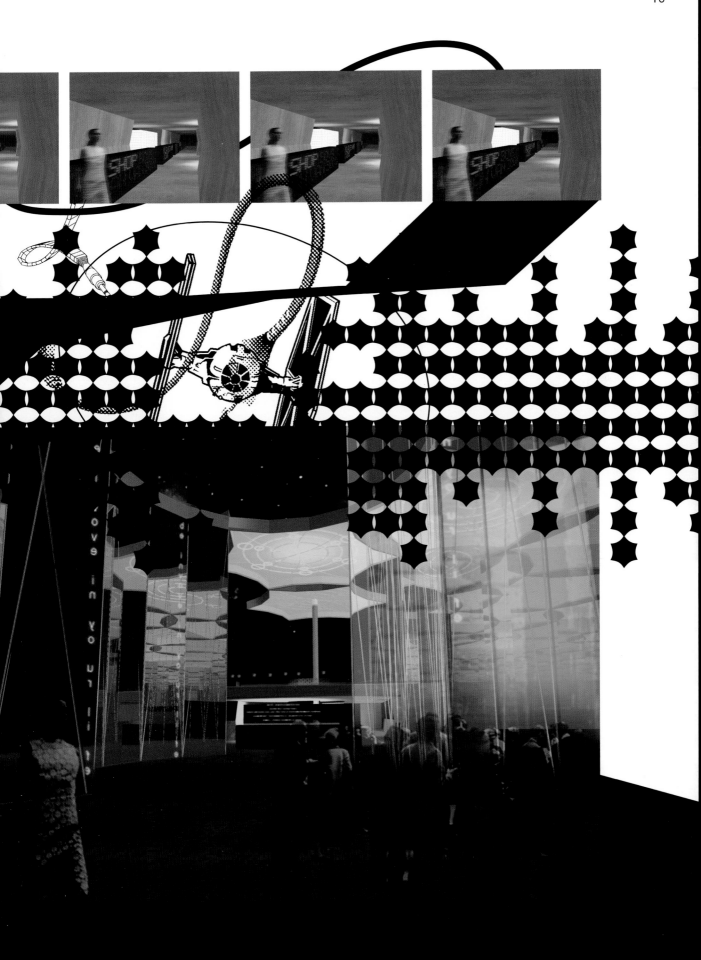

Entrance to the C.R.M.A. (regional centre for contemporary music)

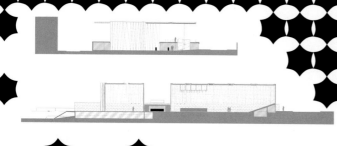

CONTEMPORARY MUSIC AUDITORIUM
Location: Nancy – France
Competition: 2002
Client: Nancy City Council
Project team: Sébastien Duron (project manager),
Yves Tougard, Stéphane Curtelin
Engineers: Khephren (structure),
Alto (building fluids)
Surface area: 2,500 m²
Cost: €5 million, incl. tax

CULTURAL PLATFORM

The brief of this project was to revitalise
a magnificent building located on the banks
of the river Seine. The underpinning design
concept involved gradually restoring the
structure to its former glory but dedicated to
contemporary artistic events, including film,
drama, dance, digital art and music.

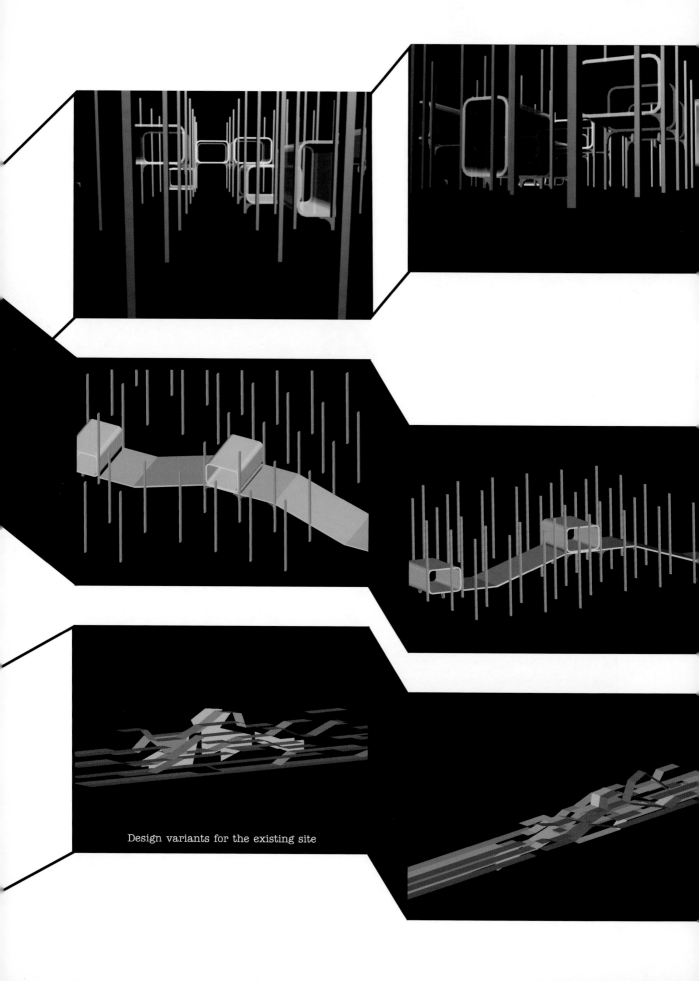

Design variants for the existing site

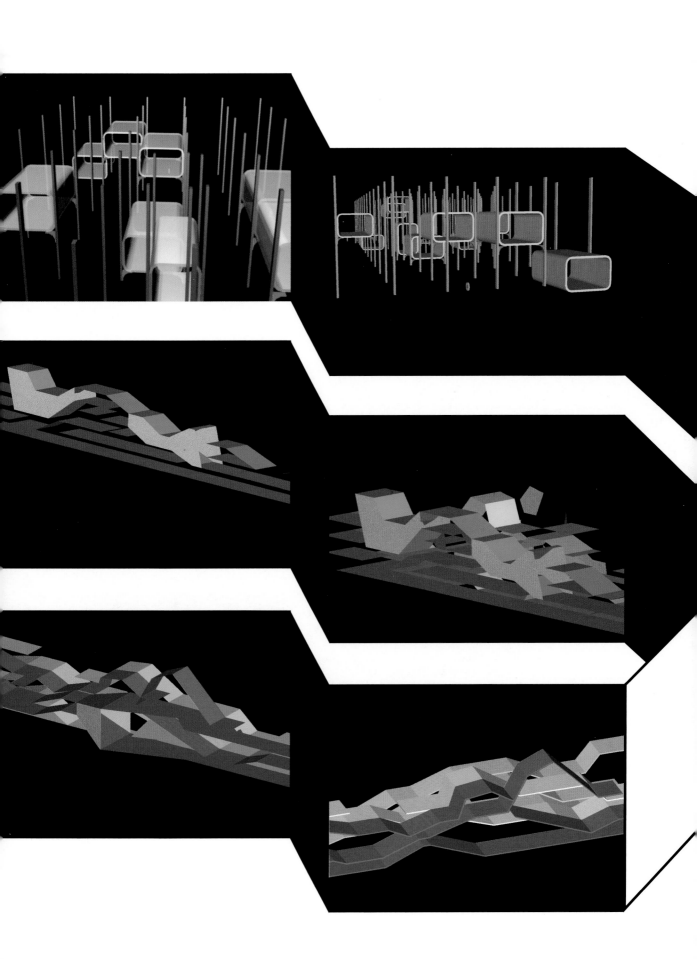

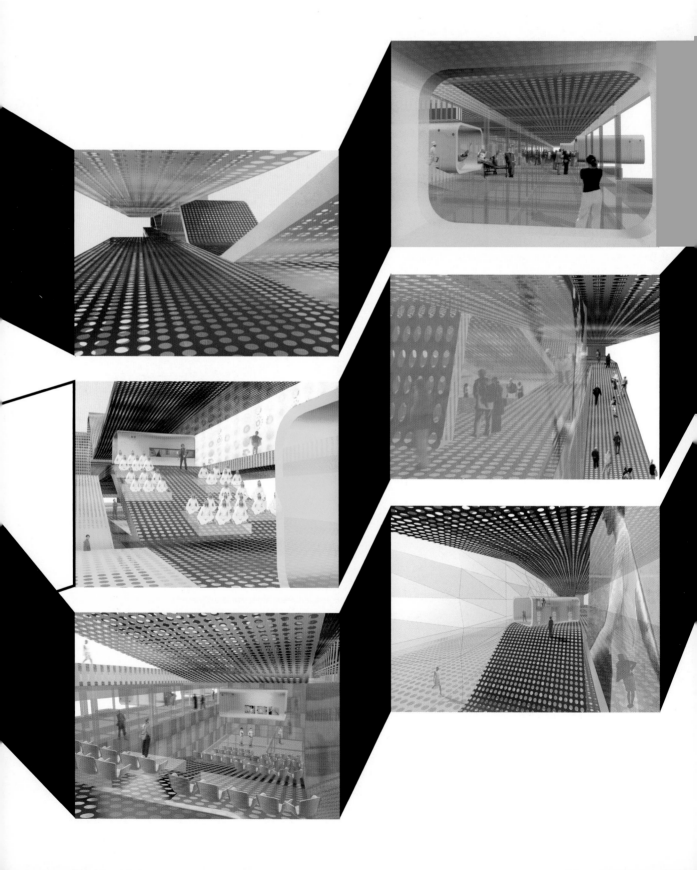

The "ribbons" fall into place, marking out the circulation paths

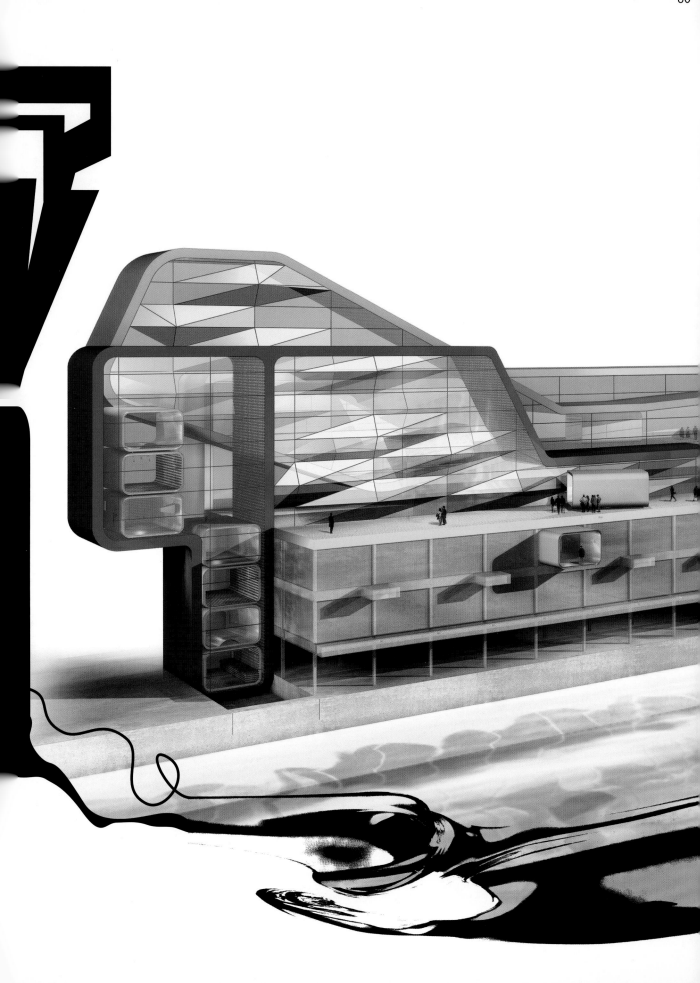

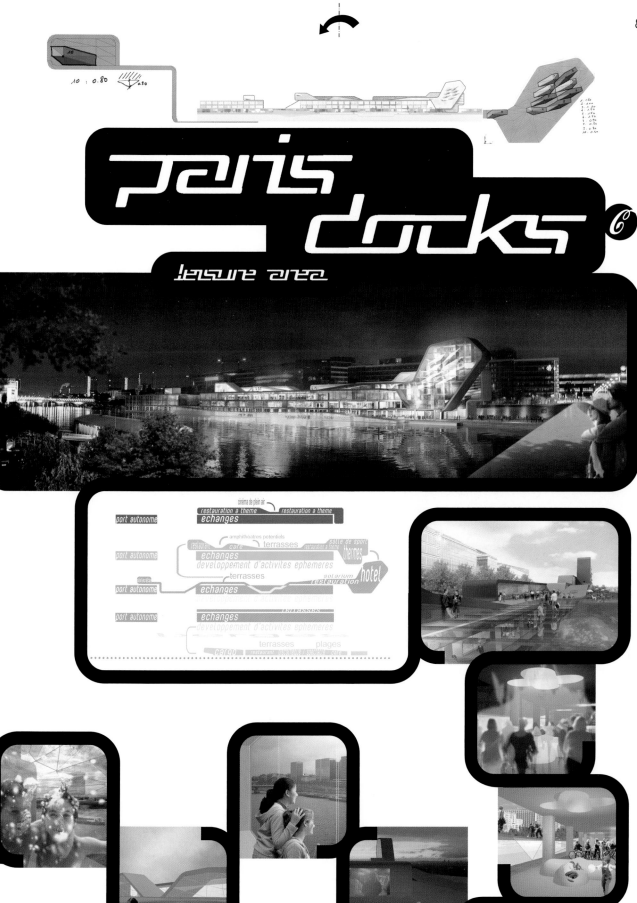

paris docks
leisure area

The *éclaireuses* can be put to various uses

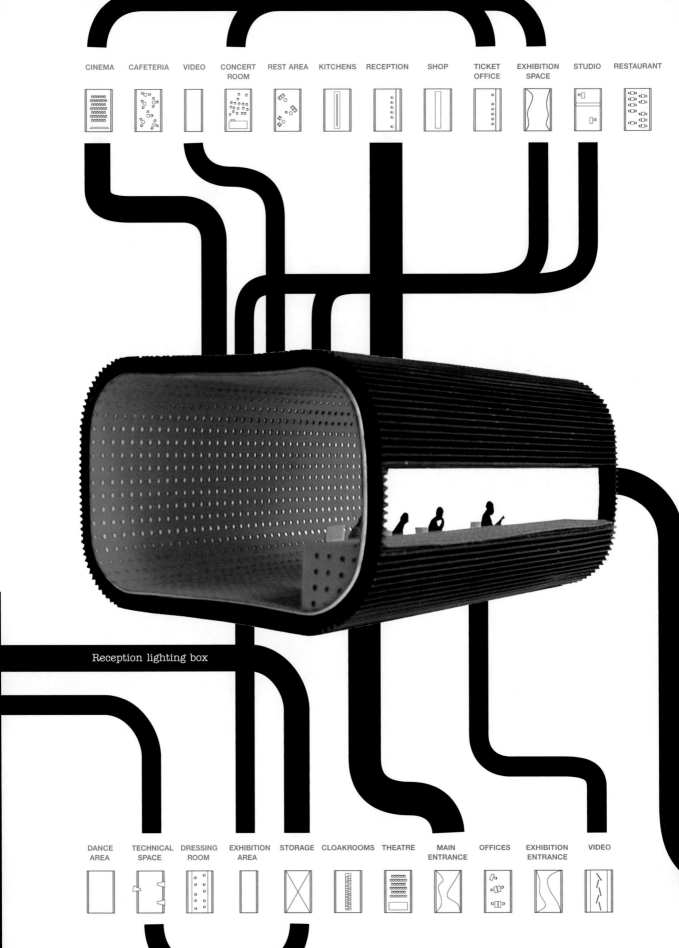

CINEMA   CAFETERIA   VIDEO   CONCERT ROOM   REST AREA   KITCHENS   RECEPTION   SHOP   TICKET OFFICE   EXHIBITION SPACE   STUDIO   RESTAURANT

Reception lighting box

DANCE AREA   TECHNICAL SPACE   DRESSING ROOM   EXHIBITION AREA   STORAGE   CLOAKROOMS   THEATRE   MAIN ENTRANCE   OFFICES   EXHIBITION ENTRANCE   VIDEO

Various uses of the lighting boxes

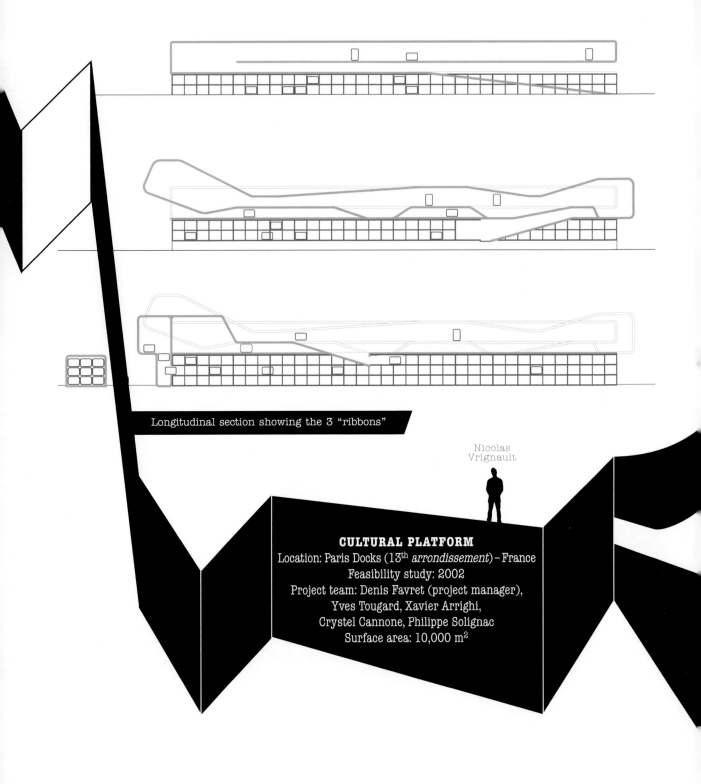

Longitudinal section showing the 3 "ribbons"

Nicolas
Vrignault

CULTURAL PLATFORM
Location: Paris Docks (13th *arrondissement*) – France
Feasibility study: 2002
Project team: Denis Favret (project manager),
Yves Tougard, Xavier Arrighi,
Crystel Cannone, Philippe Solignac
Surface area: 10,000 m²

CITROËN SHOWROOM

A wide glass dress, sculpted like origami, unfolds from one side of the site to the other, providing an infinite display of prisms, lozenges and diamond heads, as in Citroën's chevron emblem. In the centre sits a giant shelf on which eight Citroën cars can be stacked.

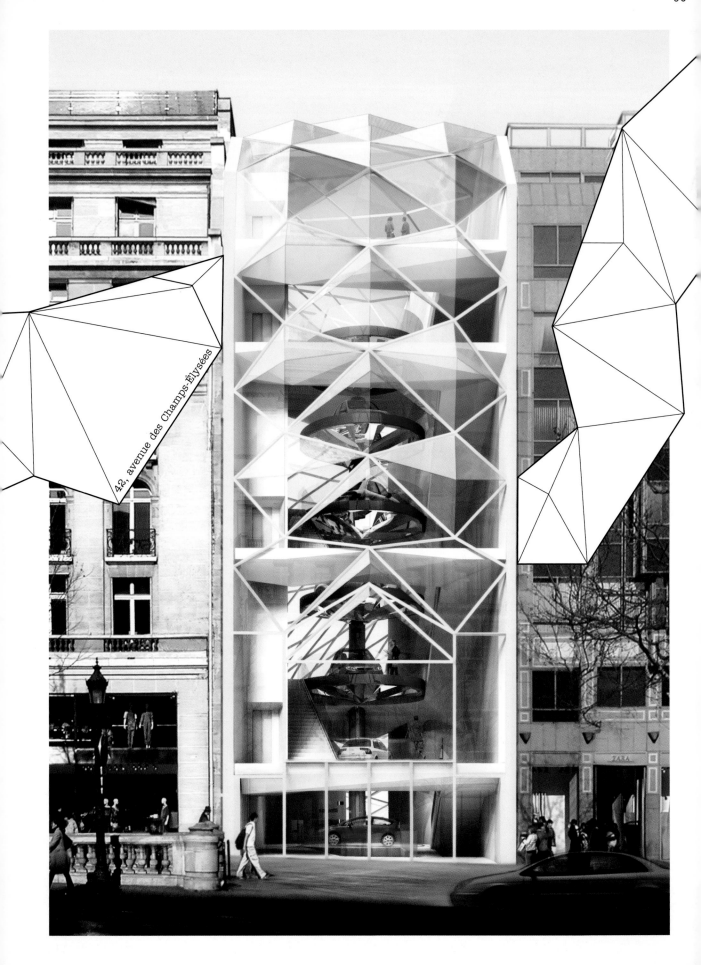

42, avenue des Champs-Élysées

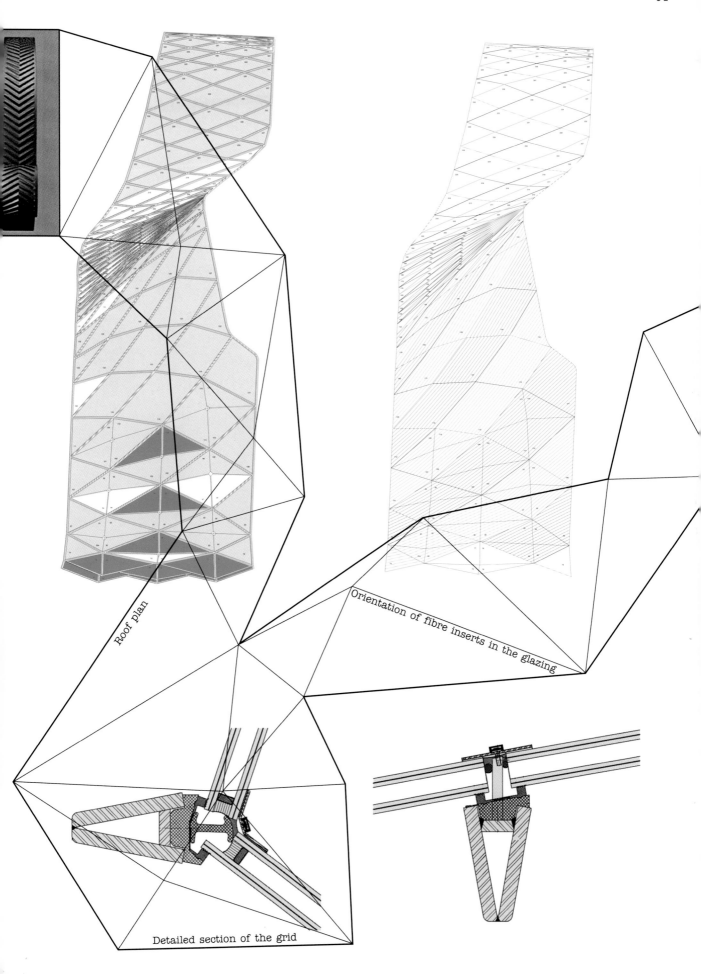

Roof plan

Orientation of fibre inserts in the glazing

Detailed section of the grid

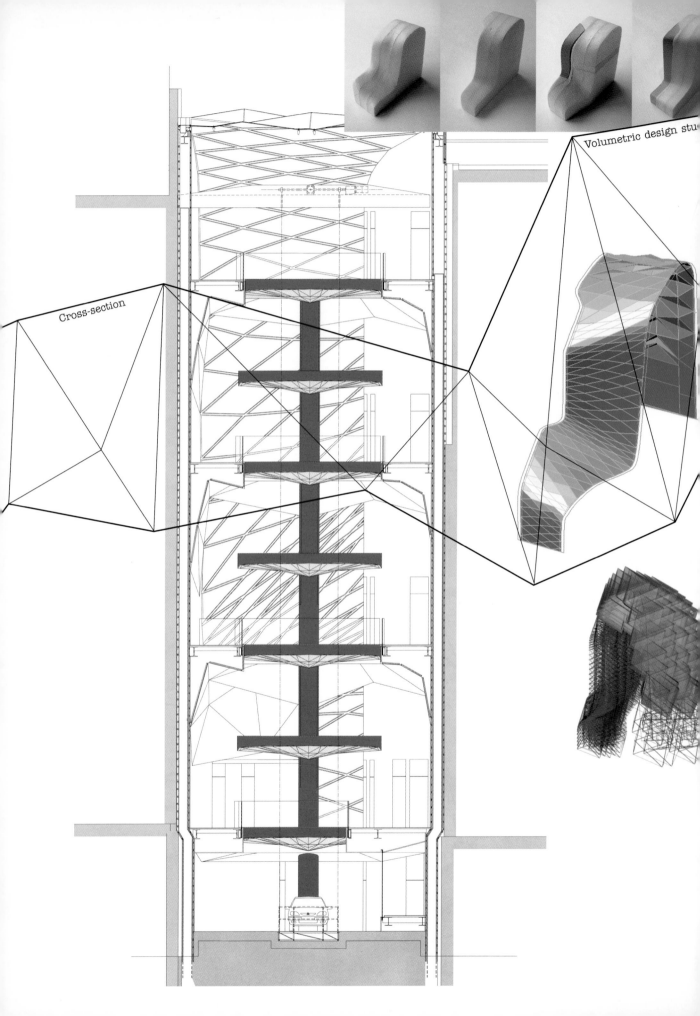

Cross-section

Volumetric design stu

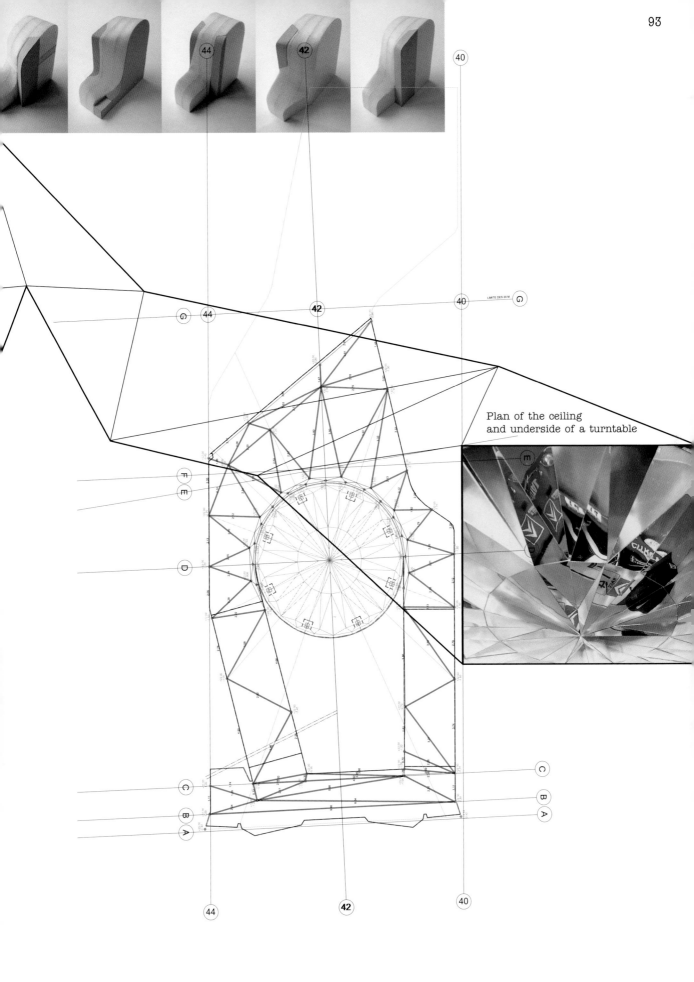

Plan of the ceiling
and underside of a turntable

93

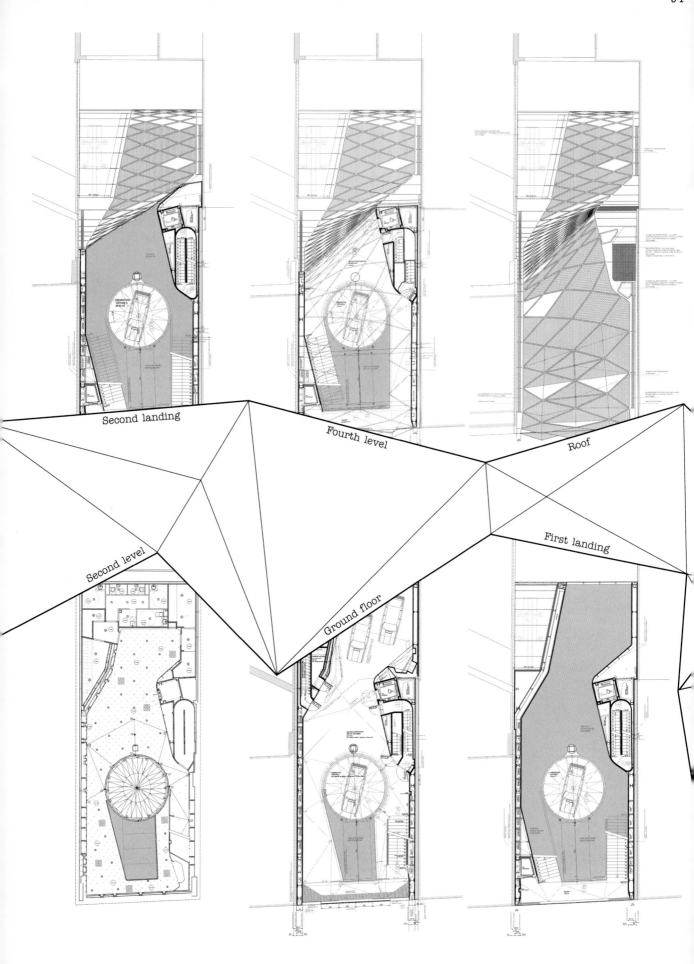

Second landing

Fourth level

Roof

Second level

First landing

Ground floor

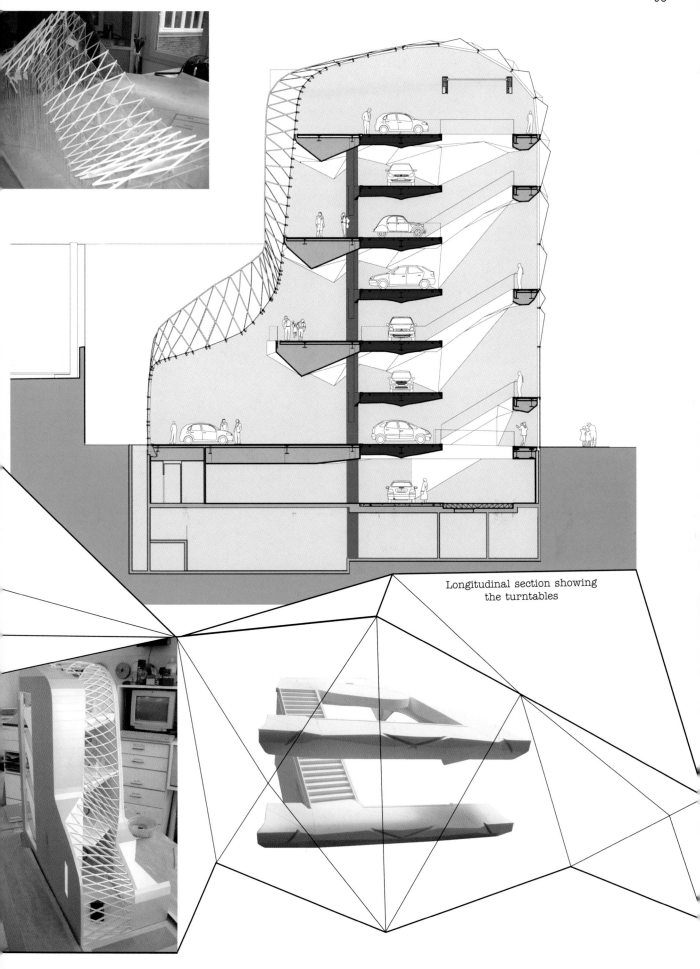

Longitudinal section showing
the turntables

95

View from the back of the showroom
towards the Champs-Élysées

IMAGE PAVILION

WU

FOR THE 2004
INTERNATIONAL EXHIBITION
IN SEINE-SAINT-DENIS

LE PROJET COMME
UN DIAMANT

PEAU EXTÉRIEURE PÉRENNE
PEAU INTÉRIEURE
(EN PARTIE ÉPHÉMÈRE)

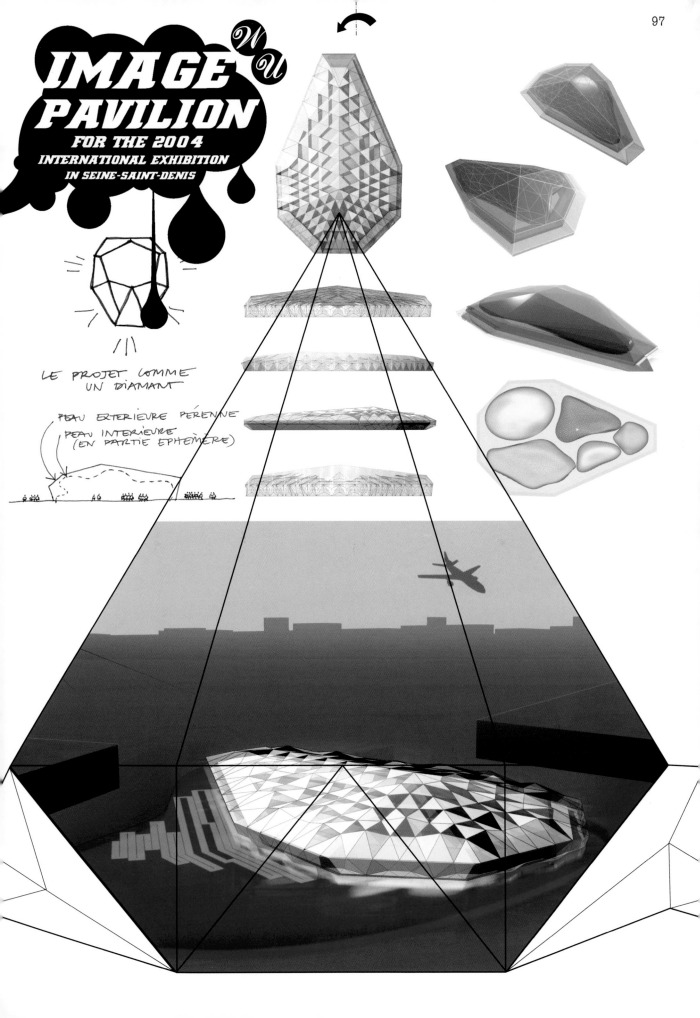

Turntable mast

Turntable mast

Marie
Duval

CITROËN SHOWROOM
Location: 42, Avenue des Champs-Elysées – Paris – France
Competition: 2002 / Estimated delivery: 2006
Client: Citroën
Project team: Anne Feldmann (project manager), Hiroo Nishiyama,
Philippe Solignac, Yves Tougard, Cédric Housset, Shirin Raissi,
Marie Duval, Miguel Silvera, Julien Roge
Engineers: Khephren (structure), A de Bussière (envelope),
Alto (building fluids), LTA (economist), Labeyrie (multimedia),
Casso (safety), Lamoureux (acoustics), Eciac (scheduling),
Spectat (mobile equipment)
Consultant: Nicolas Vrignaud (signage)
Surface area: 1,200 m²
Cost: €11 million, incl. tax

Facade prototype with
Kapipane insulation system
in the glazing and red film

HYDRO BUILDING SYSTEM STAND
AT THE BATIMAT 2003
TRADE FAIR

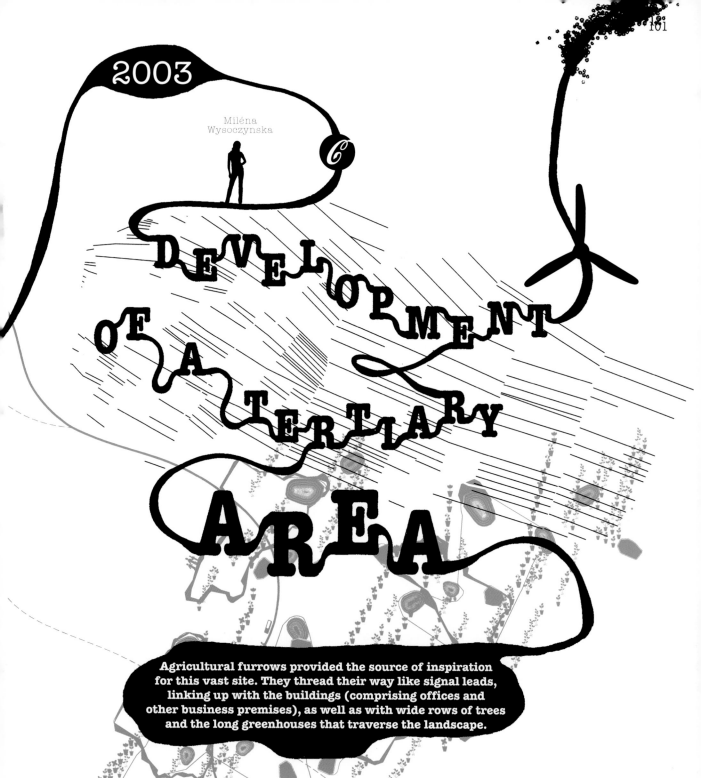

2003

Miléna
Wysoczynska

€

DEVELOPMENT
OF A TERTIARY
AREA

Agricultural furrows provided the source of inspiration
for this vast site. They thread their way like signal leads,
linking up with the buildings (comprising offices and
other business premises), as well as with wide rows of trees
and the long greenhouses that traverse the landscape.

The site is structured by the grids of the landscape

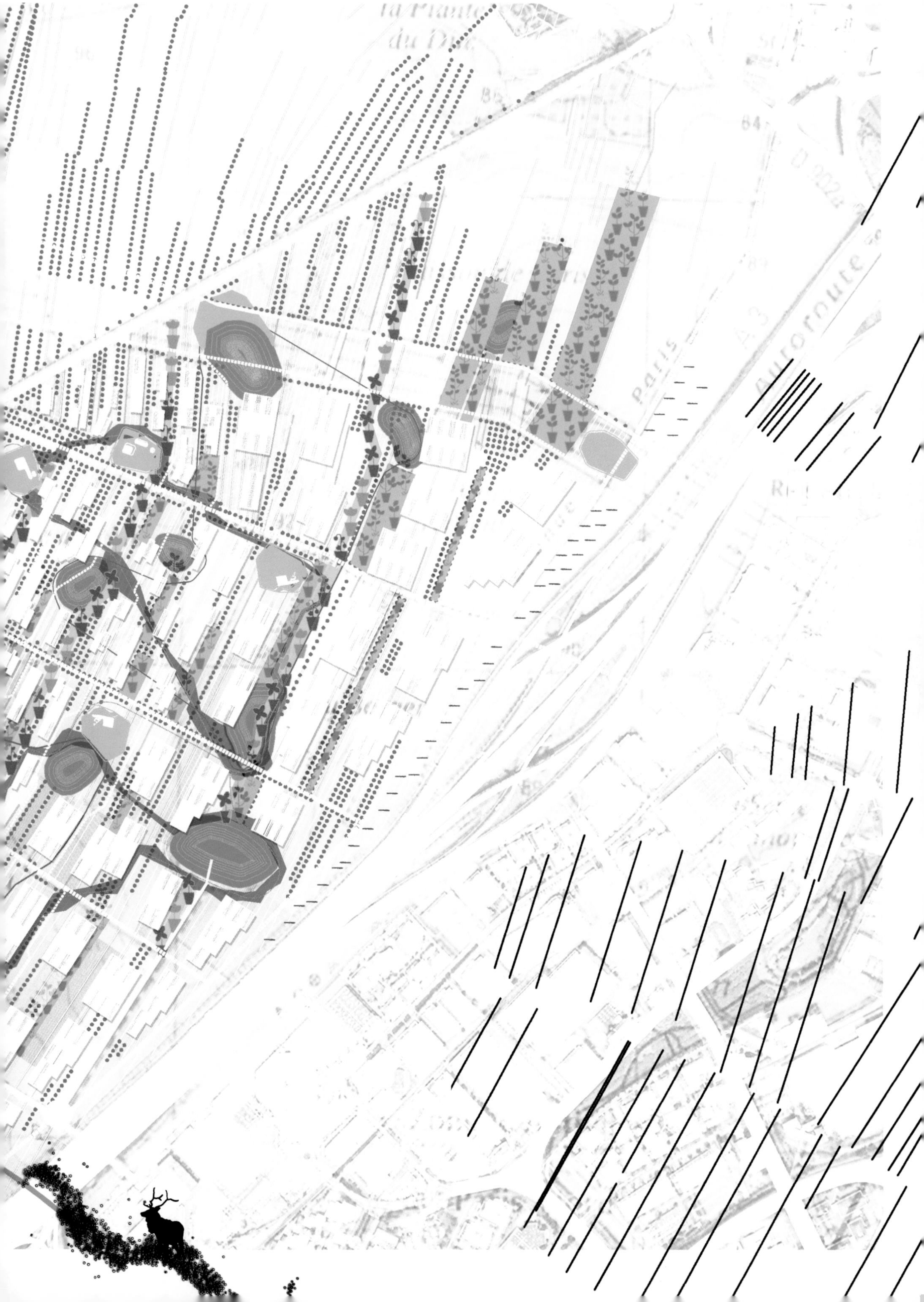
Paris
A3
Autoroute

Layout of the programmes

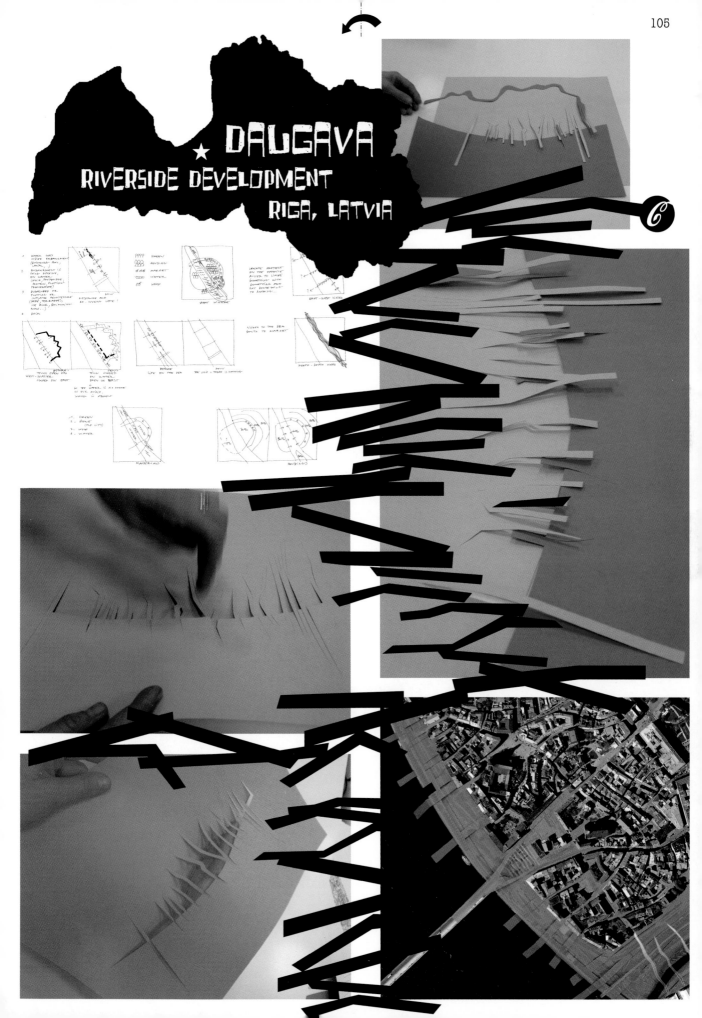

DAUGAVA
RIVERSIDE DEVELOPMENT
RIGA, LATVIA

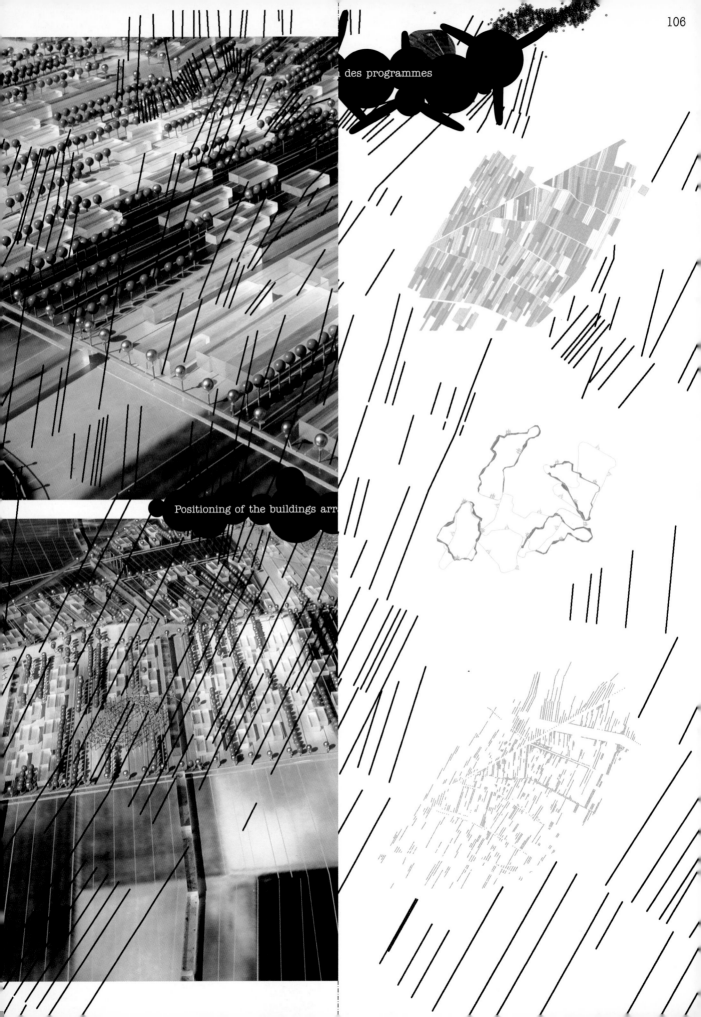

des programmes

Positioning of the buildings arr

Positioning of the buildings arranged along the furrows

Entrance to the site, through the wind turbines

TERTIARY DEVELOPMENT ZONE
Location: Paris Greater Area – France
Feasibility study: 2003-2007
Project team: Anne Feldmann (project manager),
Gaelle Leborgne, Crystel Cannone, Merav Kane
Surface area: 140 hectares

HÉLIANTHE"

Residential complex

Thirty-five high-quality apartments are stepped like stairs along the street, opening out into large south-facing terrace-gardens. The facades are decorated with a graphic motif with overlapping tones.

Merav Kane

Alexandre Dumoulin

APARTMENT BLOCK,
EURALILLE 2
(LILLE)

INTERIOR DESIGN CONCEPT
FOR BANK BRANCHES

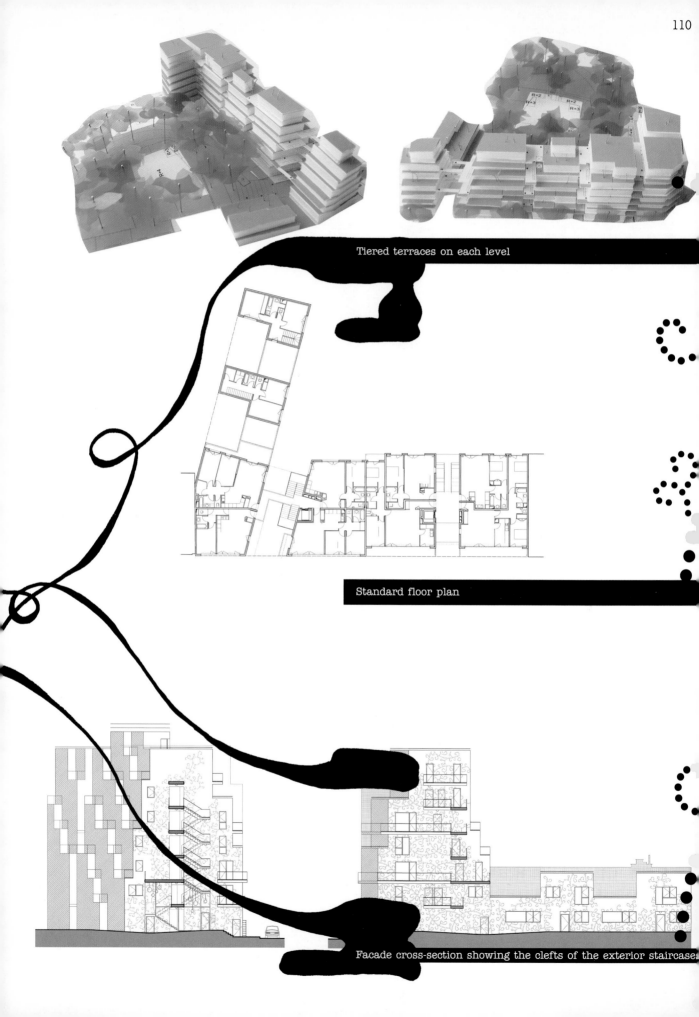

Tiered terraces on each level

Standard floor plan

Facade cross-section showing the clefts of the exterior staircase

View from the interior garden

Facade section showing the exterior staircases

RIVERSIDE
STOPPING POINT
AT FONTAINES-SUR-SÀONE

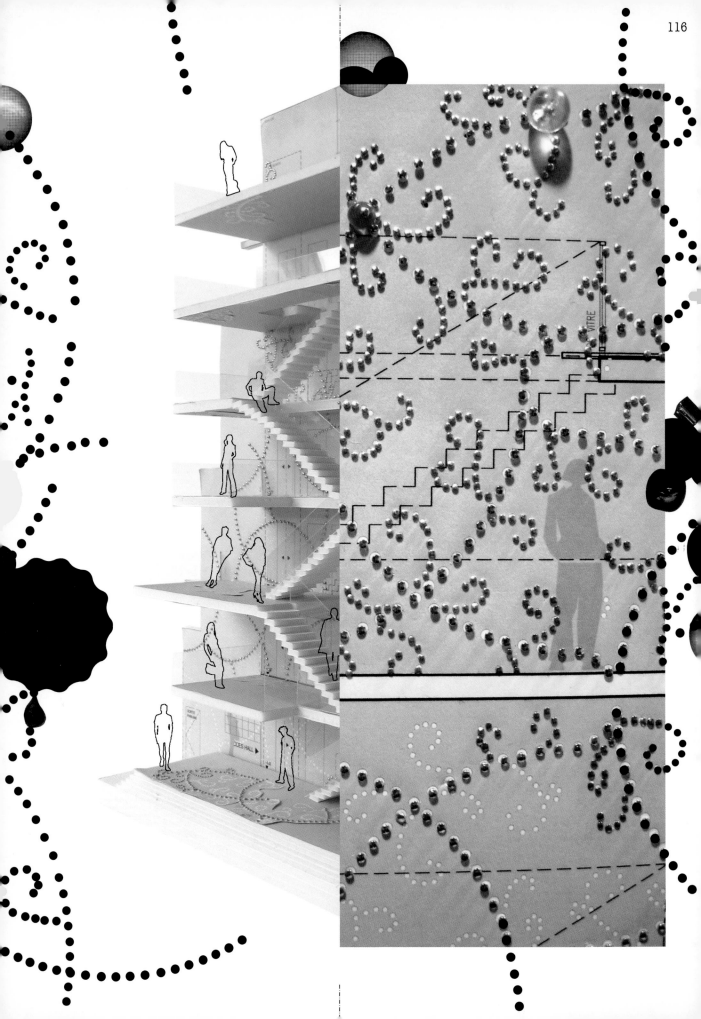

Nail head motif on the concrete

Irina
Bruscky

Selim
Mimita

HÉLIANTHE
residential complex
Location: Boulogne-Billancourt – France
Commission: 2003 / Estimated completion: 2006
Client: Capri - Sorif
Project team: Shirin Raissi (project manager), Merav Kane
Engineer: Cotec
Surface area: 3,200 m², 35 apartments
Cost: €3.8 million, incl. tax

Julien
Rogé

Julie
Nabucet

B

RESTRUCTURING AND EXTENSION OF THE LILLE MODERN ART MUSEUM

Five fan-shaped concrete folds hug the museum's existing building,
creating new exhibition spaces that house a fine collection of Art Brut.

Pleated concrete coil echoing the contours of the landscape

Entrance to the current museum (designed by the architect Roland Simounet)

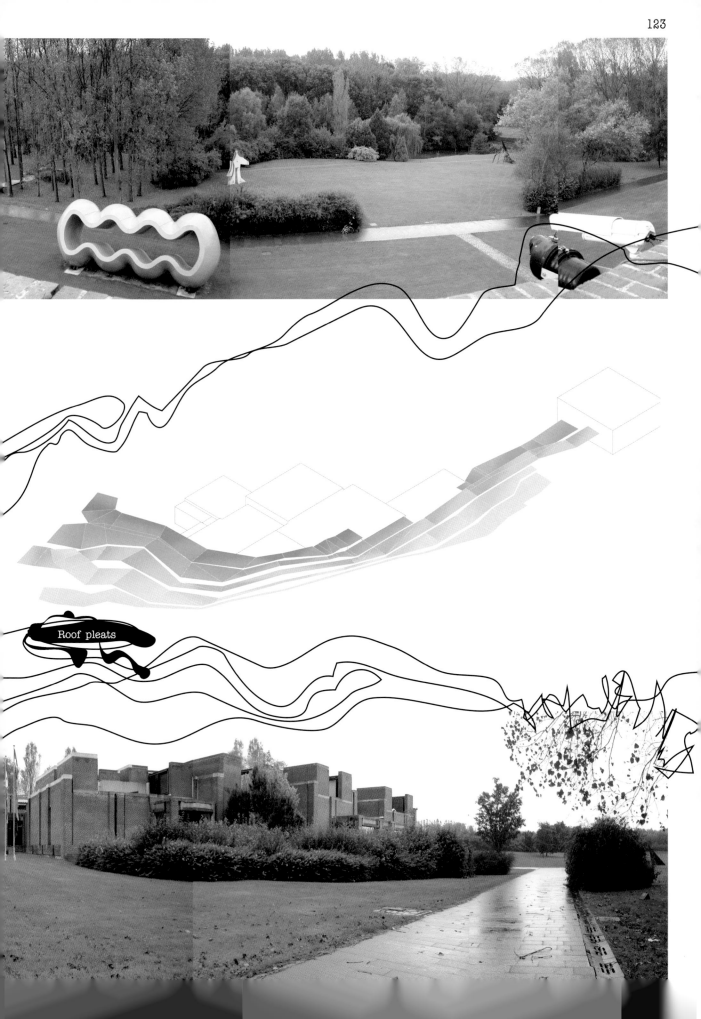

Roof pleats

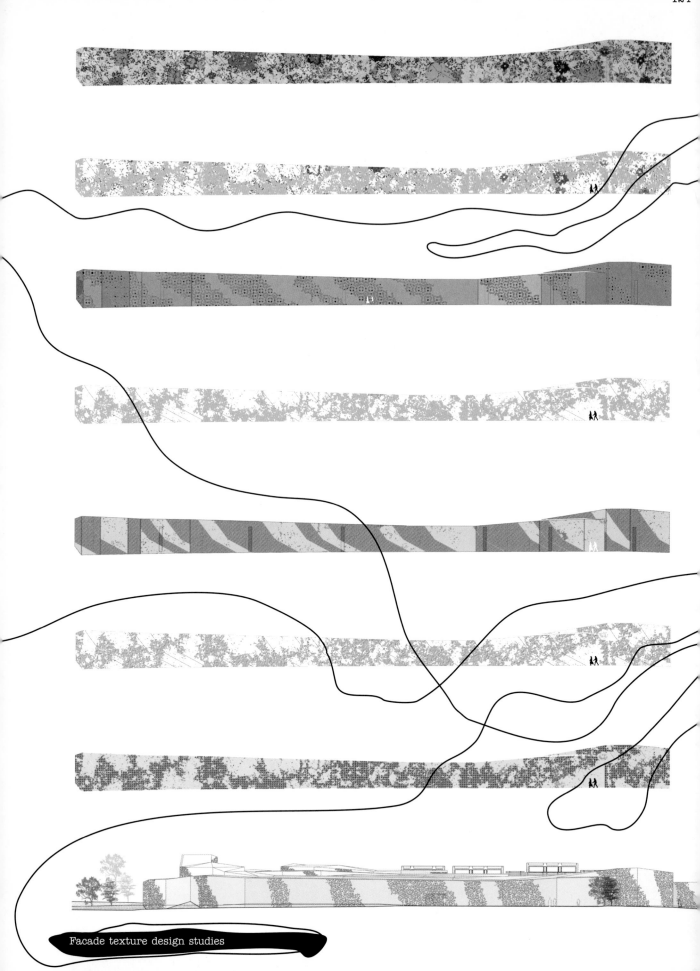

Facade texture design studies

The extension dedicated to Art Brut is wrapped around the existing Roland Simounet museum

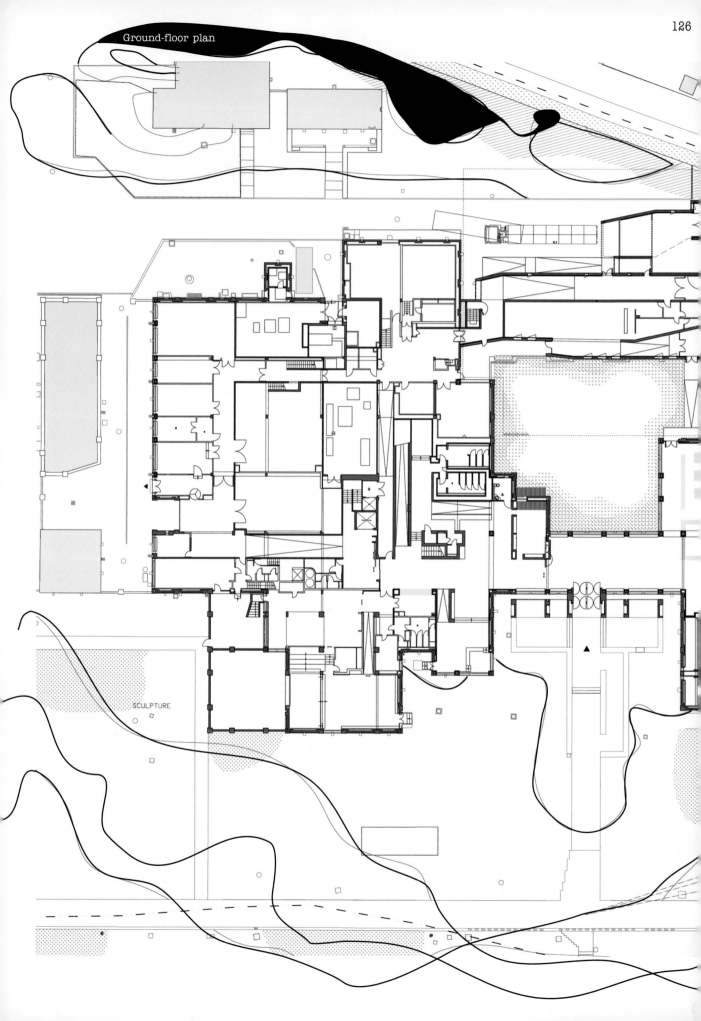

Ground-floor plan

126

SCULPTURE

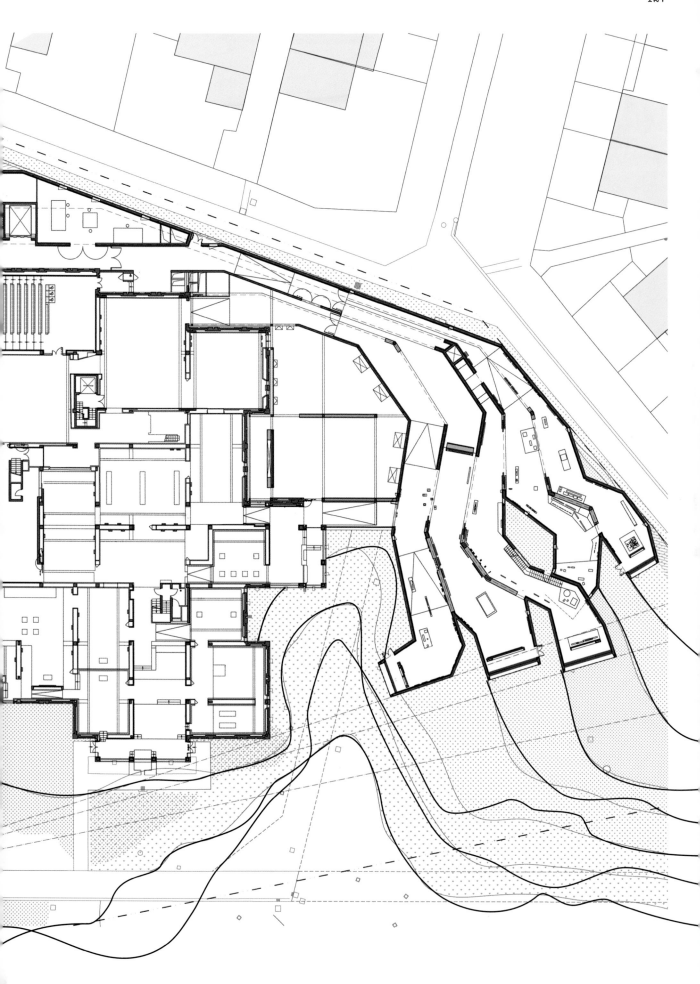

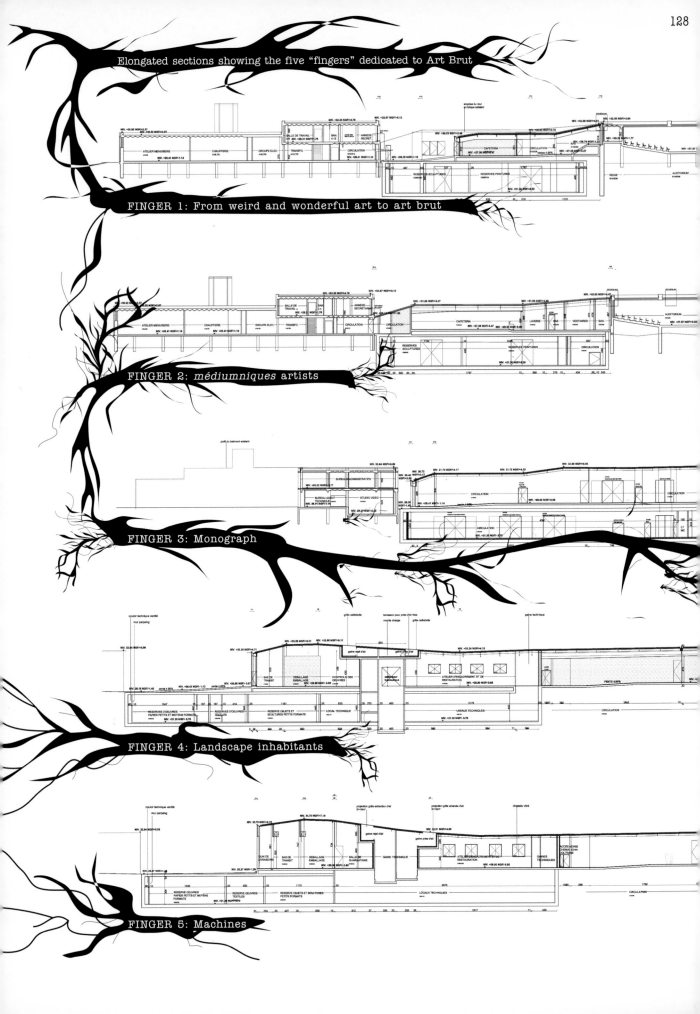

Elongated sections showing the five "fingers" dedicated to Art Brut

FINGER 1: From weird and wonderful art to art brut

FINGER 2: *médiumniques artists*

FINGER 3: Monograph

FINGER 4: Landscape inhabitants

FINGER 5: Machines

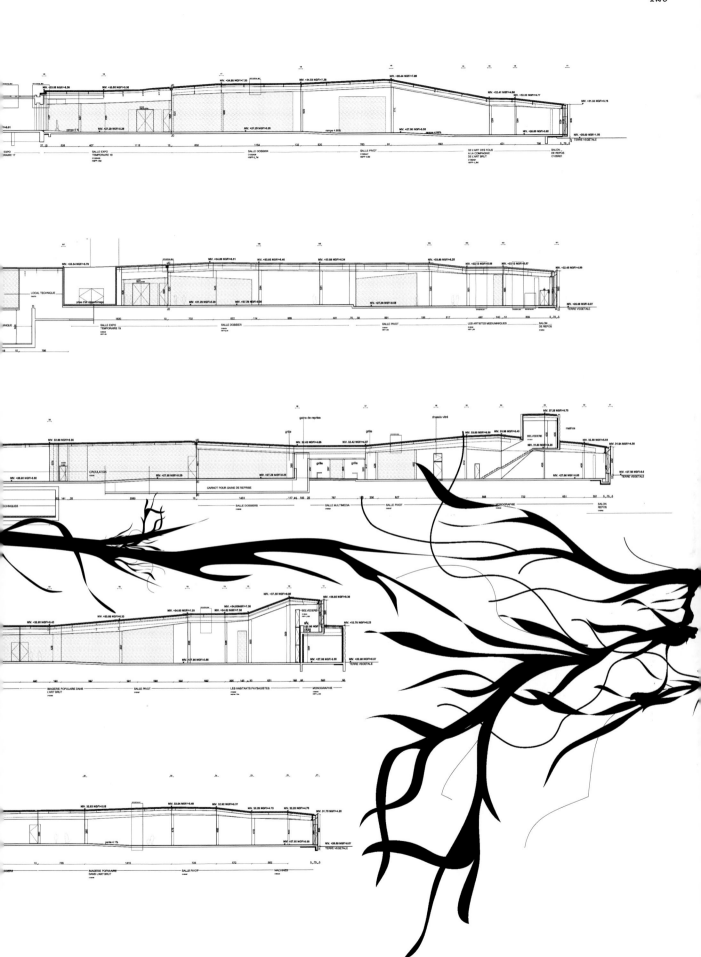

Design concept
for assembling the laced
concrete moulds

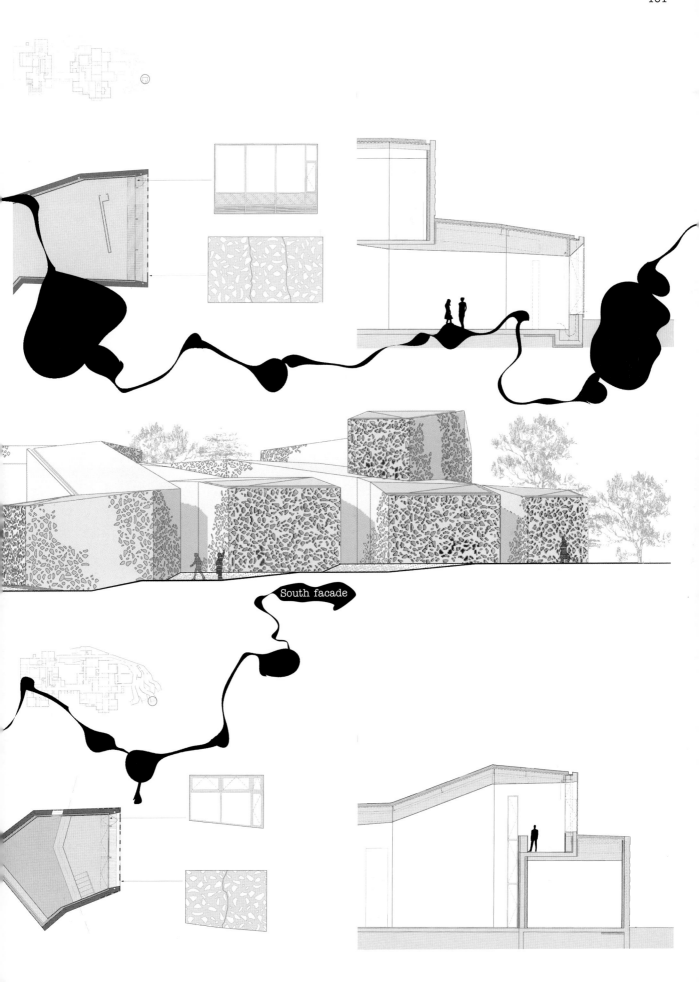

South facade

Cécile
Céleste

LILLE MODERN ART MUSEUM
Location: Allée du musée – Villeneuve d'Ascq – France
(existing museum: Rolland Simounet arch.)
Competition: 2003 / Estimated handover: 2007
Client: Communauté Urbaine de Lille
Project team: Yves Tougard (project manager), Thomas Daragon,
Maryline Gillois, Marie Duval, Merav Kane, Shirin Raissi,
Miguel Condé, Julie Nabucet, Julien Roge
Engineers: Renaud Pierard (museum layout), Khephren (structure),
Alto (building fluids), LTA (economist), Labeyrie (multimedia),
Casso (safety), Speeg & Michel (lighting)
Surface area: 9,000 m²
Cost: €11 million, incl. tax

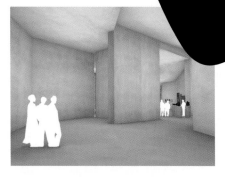
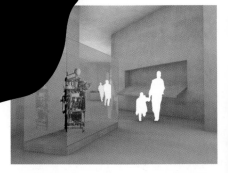

Sara
Kamalvand

Visitor circuit through the Art Brut collections

PORT STORAGE WAREHOUSE
(SAINT-NAZAIRE)

CITROËN STAND
FOR THE MADRID
MOTOR SHOW

2004

Frédéric
Arnoult

Fanny
Orihuela

Gaëlle
Le Borgne

Mathilde
Tournyol du Clos

Sandrine
Puech

Maryline
Gillois

Ouaffa
Messaoudi

Cristina
Devizzi

LA GAÎTÉ LYRIQUE

Centre dedicated to contemporary music and interactive arts

Here, digital art and contemporary music have taken over from operetta. The design underpinning the recycled structure is daring, with modular exhibition spaces and concert rooms that enable artists and the public to mix.

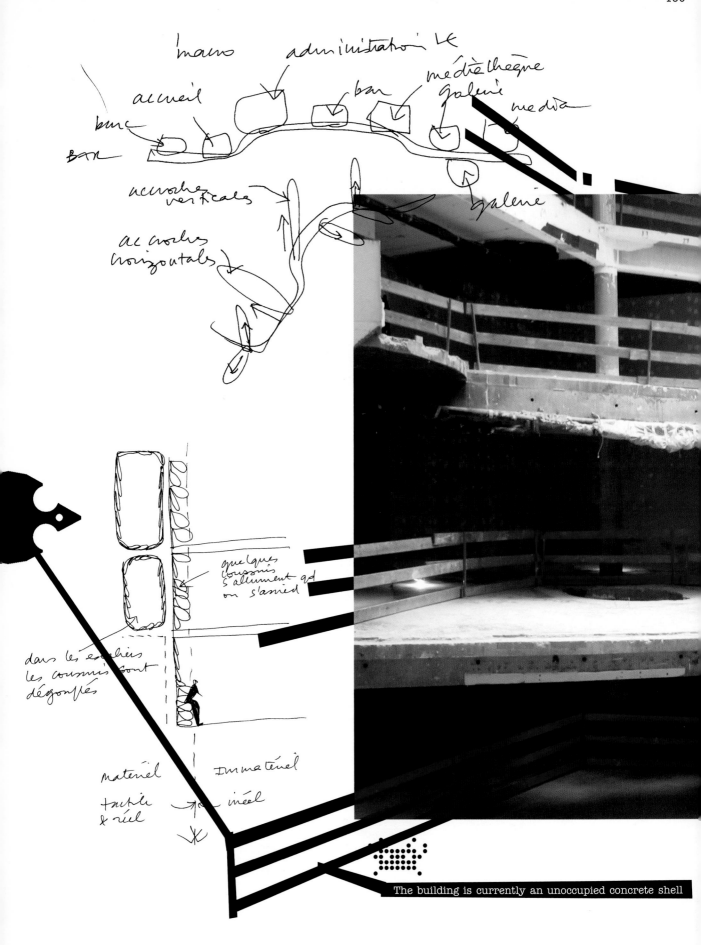

The building is currently an unoccupied concrete shell

par à géométrie
variable en
hauteur d' en longeur

Stacked design elements
of the programme

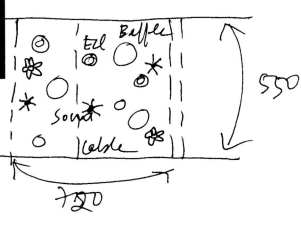

550

720

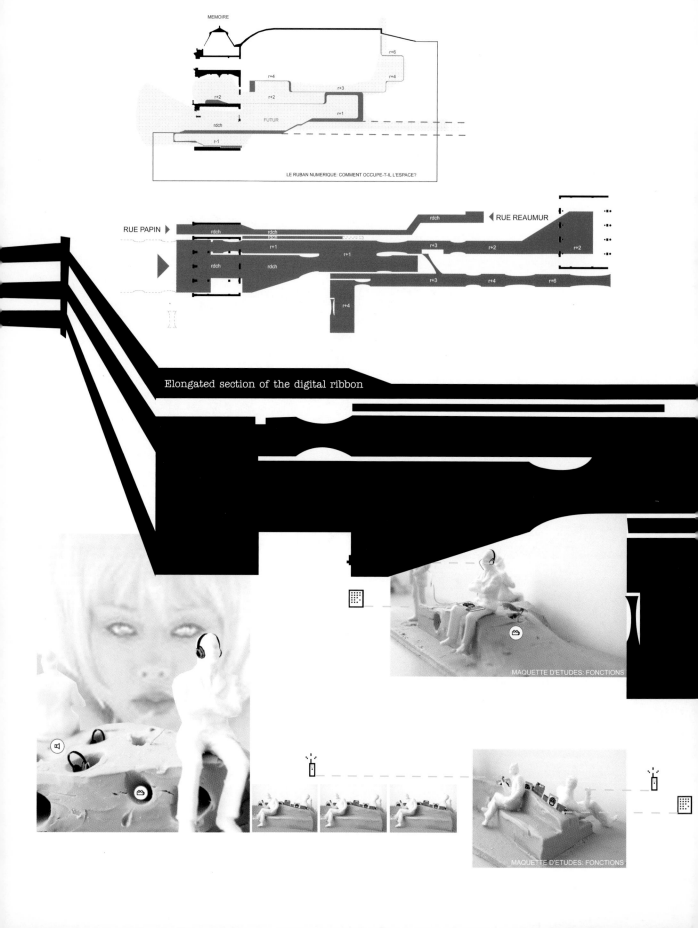

MEMOIRE

r+6
r+4
r+4
r+3
r+2
r+2
r+2
r+1

rdch
FUTUR

r-1

LE RUBAN NUMERIQUE: COMMENT OCCUPE-T-IL L'ESPACE?

RUE PAPIN ▶

rdch

rdch
rdch

◀ RUE REAUMUR

rdch

r+1
r+1
r+3
r+2
r+2

rdch
rdch

r+3
r+4
r+6

r+4

Elongated section of the digital ribbon

MAQUETTE D'ETUDES: FONCTIONS

MAQUETTE D'ETUDES: FONCTIONS

The digital ribbon acts a support for the multimedia equipment

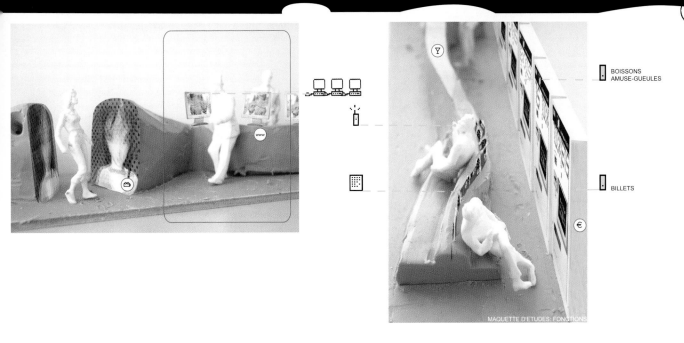

www

BOISSONS
AMUSE-GUEULES

BILLETS

€

MAQUETTE D'ETUDES: FONCTIONS

Standard polyurethane module of the digital ribbon

The ribbon lays out the visitor path

Library modules

Reception modules

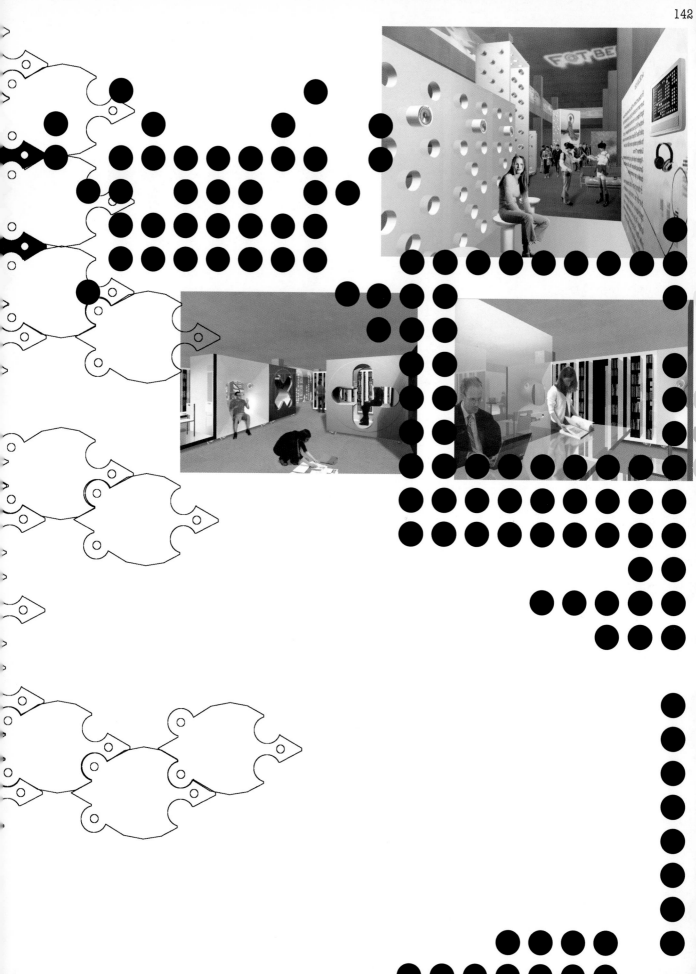

Lighting boxes in the multi-media library

Design typology
of the *éclaireuses*
(initial version)

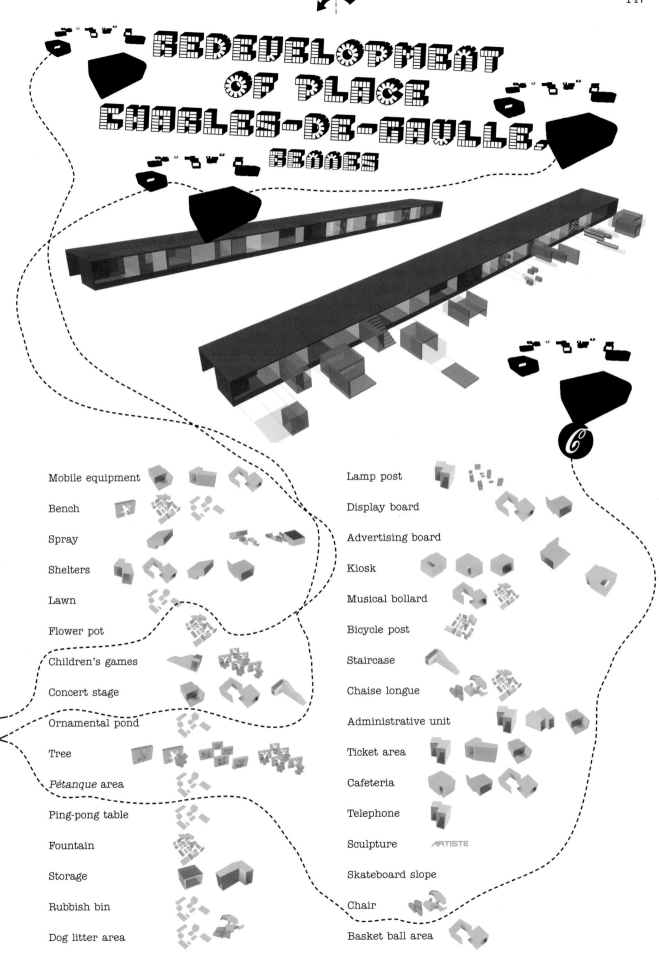

REDEVELOPMENT OF PLACE GNABLES-DE-GAULLE, RENNES

Mobile equipment

Bench

Spray

Shelters

Lawn

Flower pot

Children's games

Concert stage

Ornamental pond

Tree

Pétanque area

Ping-pong table

Fountain

Storage

Rubbish bin

Dog litter area

Lamp post

Display board

Advertising board

Kiosk

Musical bollard

Bicycle post

Staircase

Chaise longue

Administrative unit

Ticket area

Cafeteria

Telephone

Sculpture   ARTISTE

Skateboard slope

Chair

Basket ball area

Design typology
of the *éclaireuses*
(initial version)

Design typology
of the *éclaireuses*
(final version)

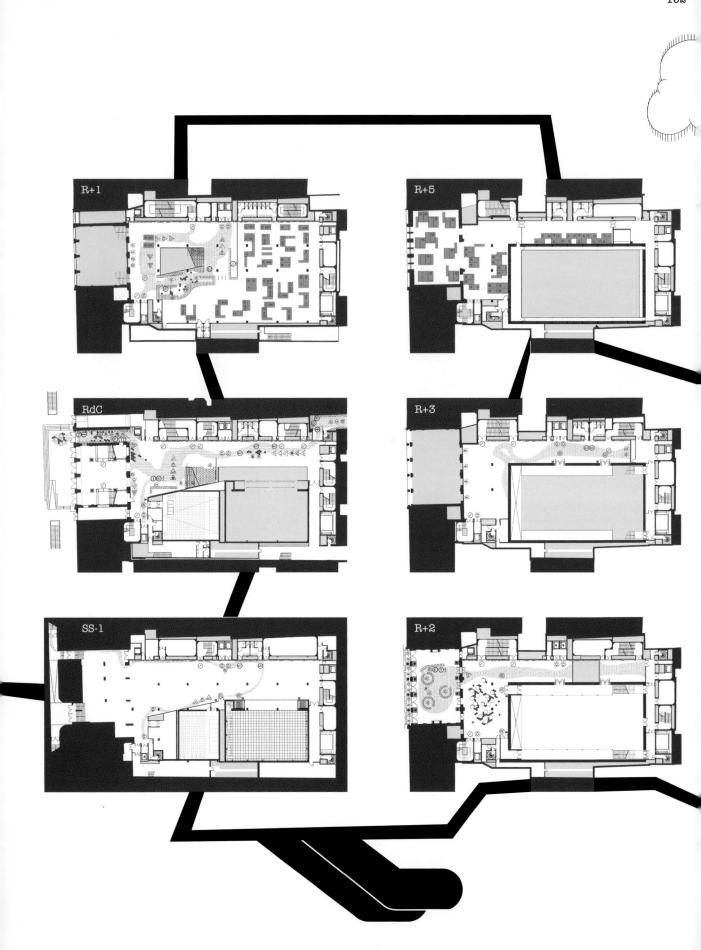

153

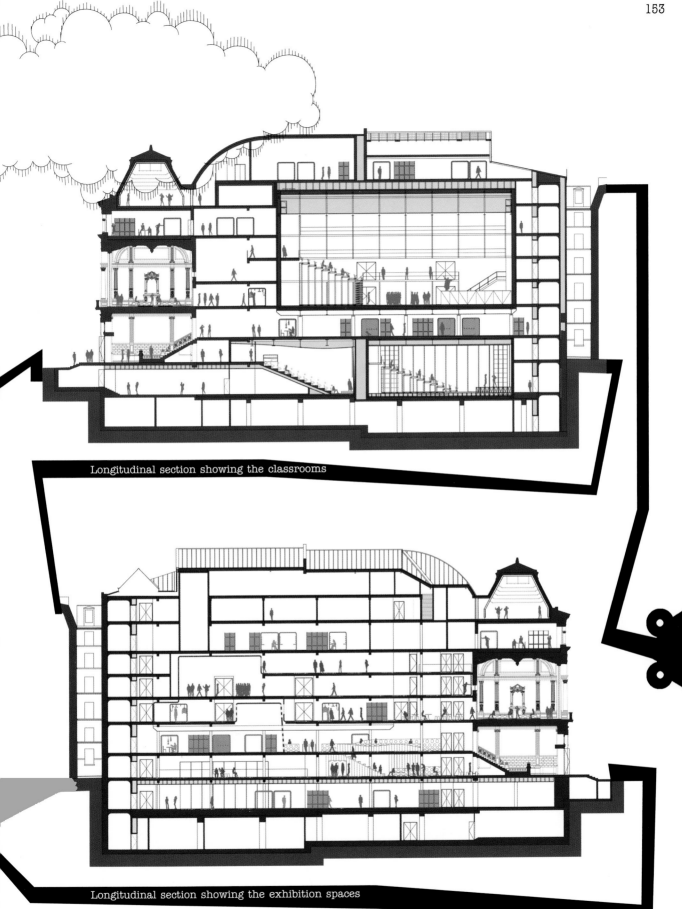

Longitudinal section showing the classrooms

Longitudinal section showing the exhibition spaces

Media lighting boxes in the multimedia library

LA GAÎTÉ LYRIQUE

Location: Rue Papin – Paris (3rd *arrondissement*) – France
Competition: 2003 / Estimated handover: 2007
Client: Paris City Council
Project team: Frédéric Arnoult (project manager), Marie Duval, Frédéric Caudoux,
Miléna Wysoczynska, Fannie Orihuela, Mathilde Tournyol du Clos, Analia Garcia,
Anna Szczeklik, Anna Pujdak, Cristina Devizzi, Bertrand Colson, Philippe Solignac,
Maryline Gillois, Hiroo Nishiyama, Yves Tougard, Hendrik van Boetzelaer,
Merav Kane, Xavier Arrighi, Julie Nabucet
Engineers: Régis Grima (historic building), OTH (general engineering),
Jean-Paul Chabert (scenography), Tisseyre (acoustics),
LTA (economist), Labeyrie (multimedia), Casso (safety),
Pro-développement (programming)
Consultants: Isabelle Chaigne (contemporary music),
Mathieu Marguerin (digital arts), Nicolas Vrignault (signage),
Surface area: 11,000 m²
Cost: €45 million, incl. tax

𝒞
PSA OFFICE BUILDING
(VÉLIZY - FRANCE)

𝒞
RECONSTRUCTION OF THE AVARICUM
DISTRICT COMPRISING APARTMENTS,
HOTEL AND SHOPS
(BOURGES - FRANCE)

Thomas
Daragon

CASINO HEADQUARTER

Roof pleats

A dozen buildings sit in orderly rows, perched
like a flock of birds, housing the new headquarters
of the Casino Group. The site is designed in the form
of a multitude of house-type offices, joined
to one another around patio-gardens.

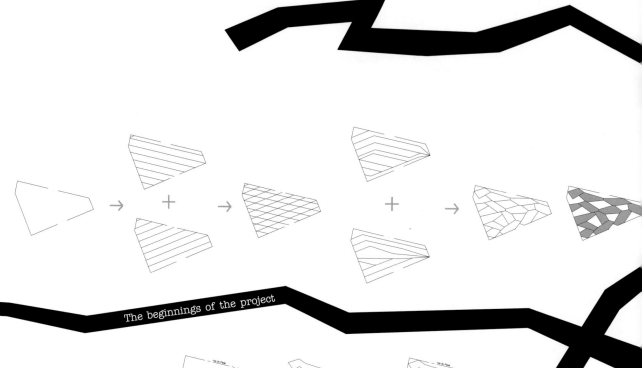

The beginnings of the project

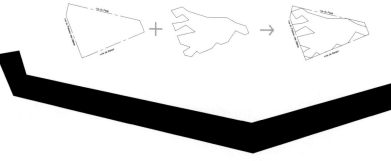

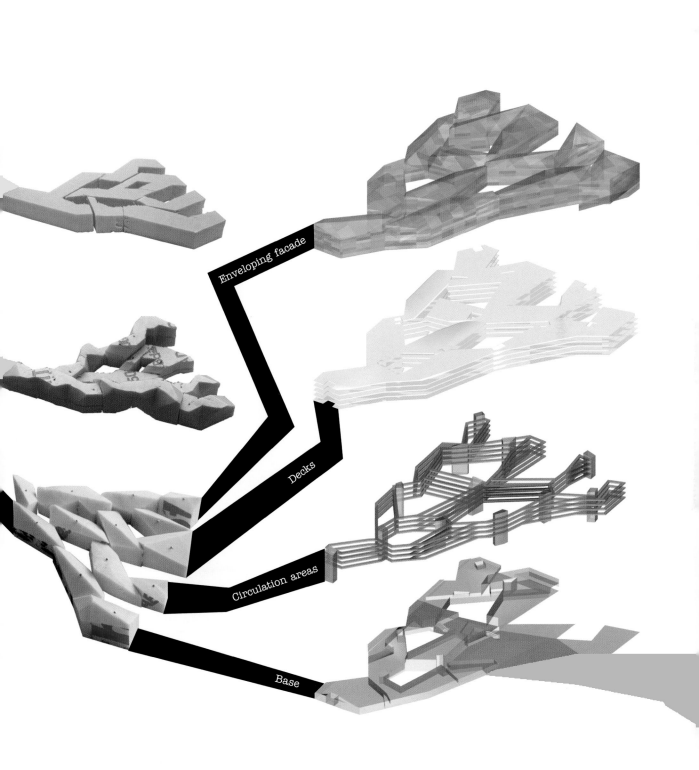

Enveloping facade

Decks

Circulation areas

Base

House-type offices appropriate the site

CINEMA
AT
ANTHONY

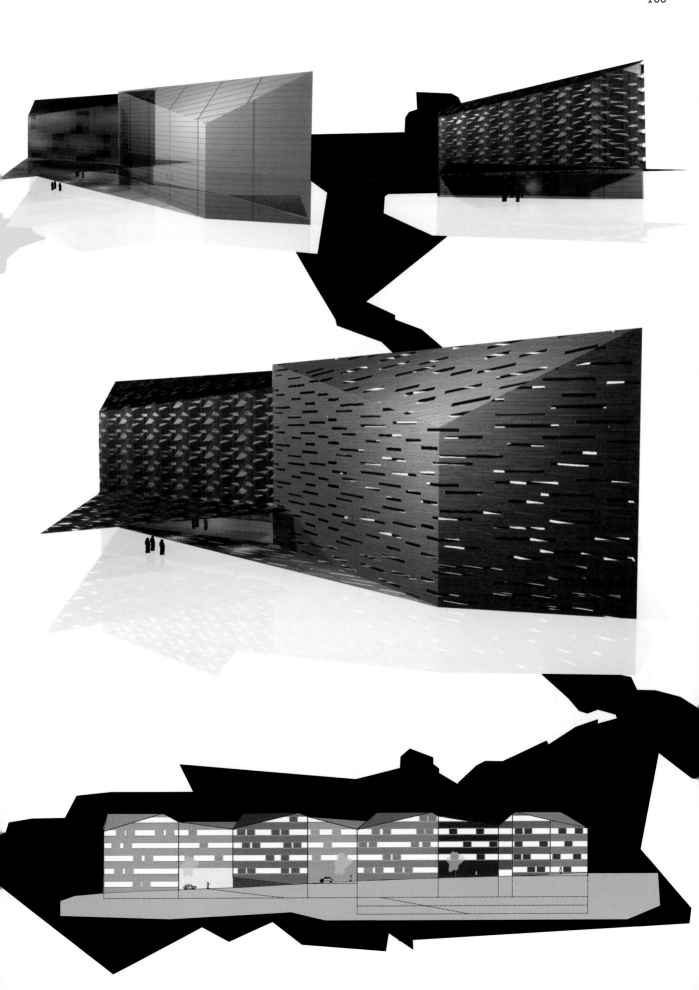

Pauline
Thierry

Benjamin
Clarens

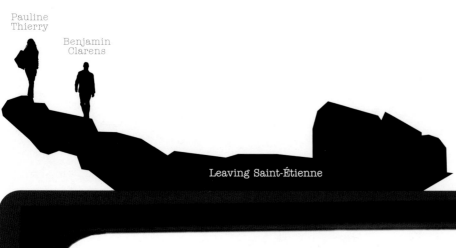

Leaving Saint-Étienne

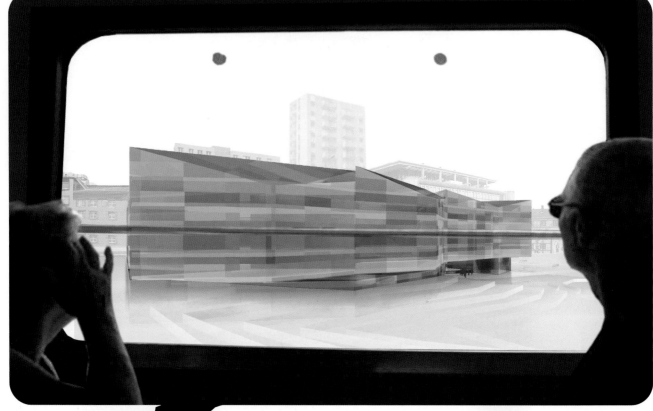

Jean-Marc
Rio

ENVELOPING FACADE, ILE SEGUIN
(BOULOGNE-BILLANCOURT - FRANCE)

CASINO HEADQUARTERS
Location: Châteaucreux quarter – Saint-Etienne – France
Competition: 2004
Client: Casino Group
Project team: Thomas Daragon (project manager),
Yves Tougard, Bertrand Colson
Engineers: Arcora (facades), Khephren (structure),
Alto (building fluids), LTA (economist),
Casso (safety)
Surface area: 55,000 m²
Cost: €65 million, incl. tax

Bertrand
Colson

R

LA PLACE NAUTIQUE

Residential complex

Pantéa
Bahiraie

The apartments are set out in three plots containing one building per architect (Agence Gautrand, MVRDV and Erick Van Egeraat). The overall design forms three wings stretching out in staggered arrangement towards the horizon in order to effectively capture the site's magnificent views over the river Saône.

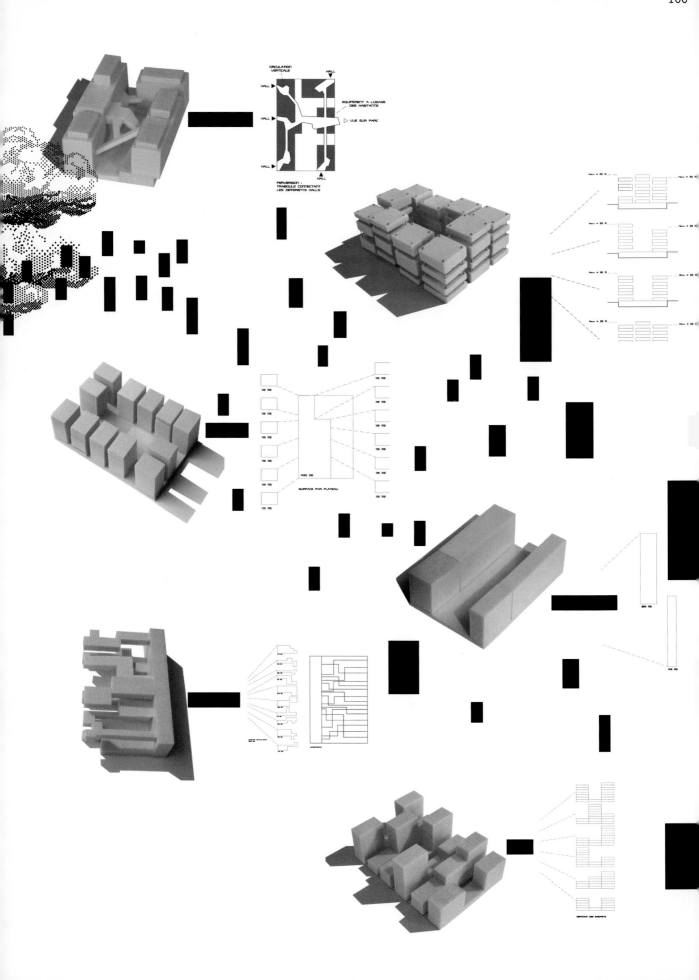

Solids and voids

Study into vertical forms

West facade overlooking the river Saône

View of plot A from the river Saône

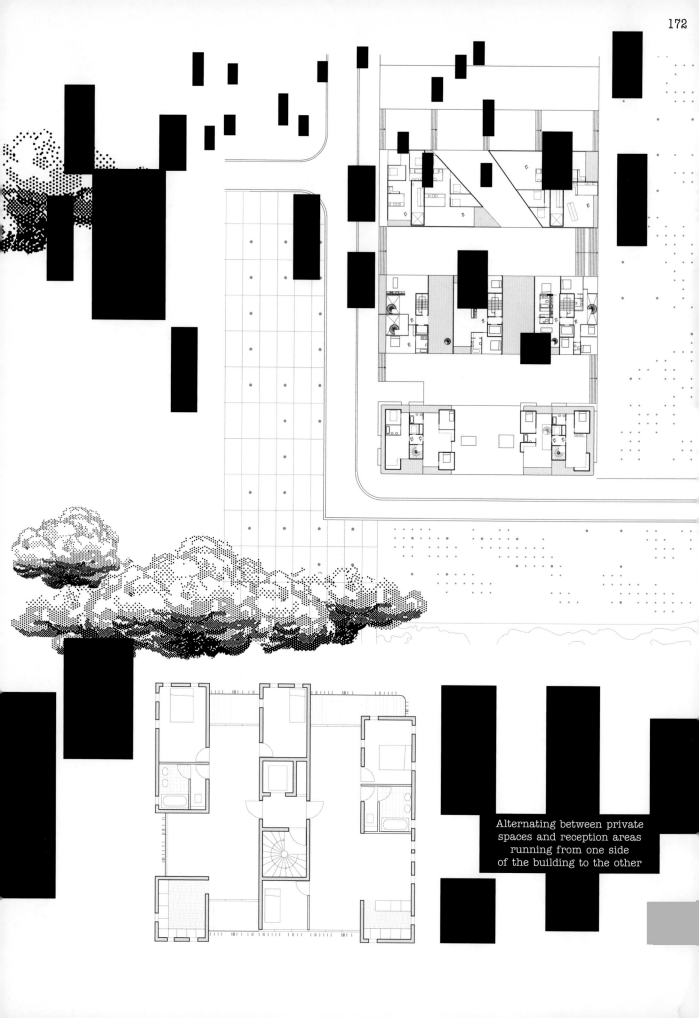

Alternating between private
spaces and reception areas
running from one side
of the building to the other

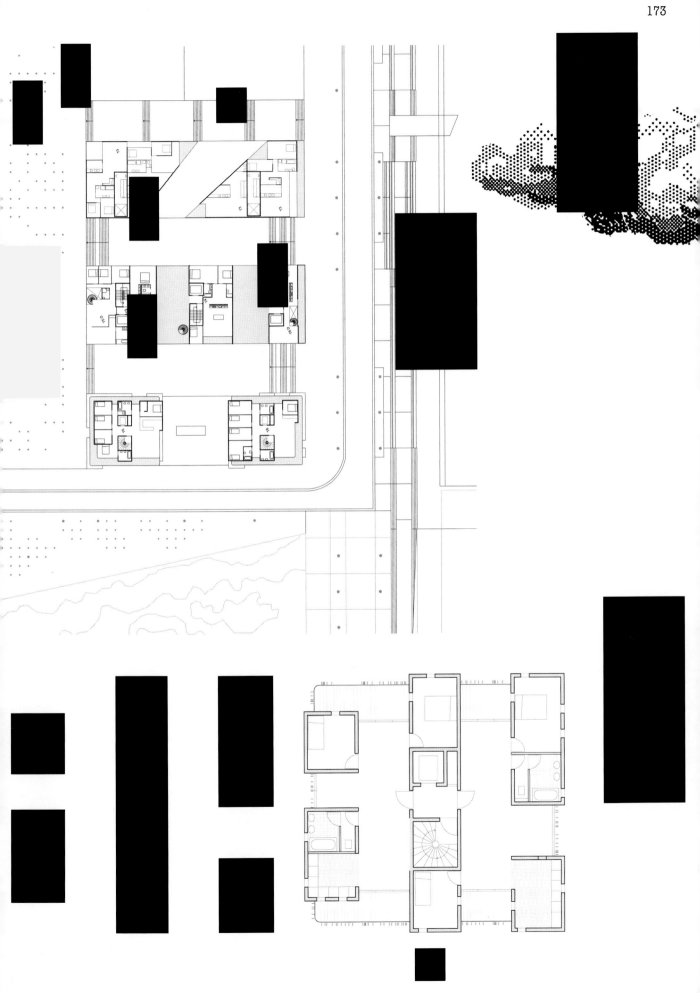

LA PLACE NAUTIQUE
Residential complex
Location: Lyon-Confluence quarter – Lyon – France
Competition: 2004
Client: ING and Atemi
Project team: Bertrand Colson (project manager),
Thomas Daragon, Yves Tougard, Maryline Gillois
Engineers: Khephren (structure), Alto (building fluids)
Surface area: 9,000 m², 60 apartments
Cost: €11 million, incl. tax

B LYON
CONFLUENCE
Office buildings

This project was designed by five teams of architects:
MVRDV, Erick Van Egeraat, Pierre Gauthier, Emmanuel
Combarel/Dominique Marrec and ourselves. It was first
of all devised as a monolith, before being divided into five
precise, different sequences, with one sequence
dedicated to each architect.

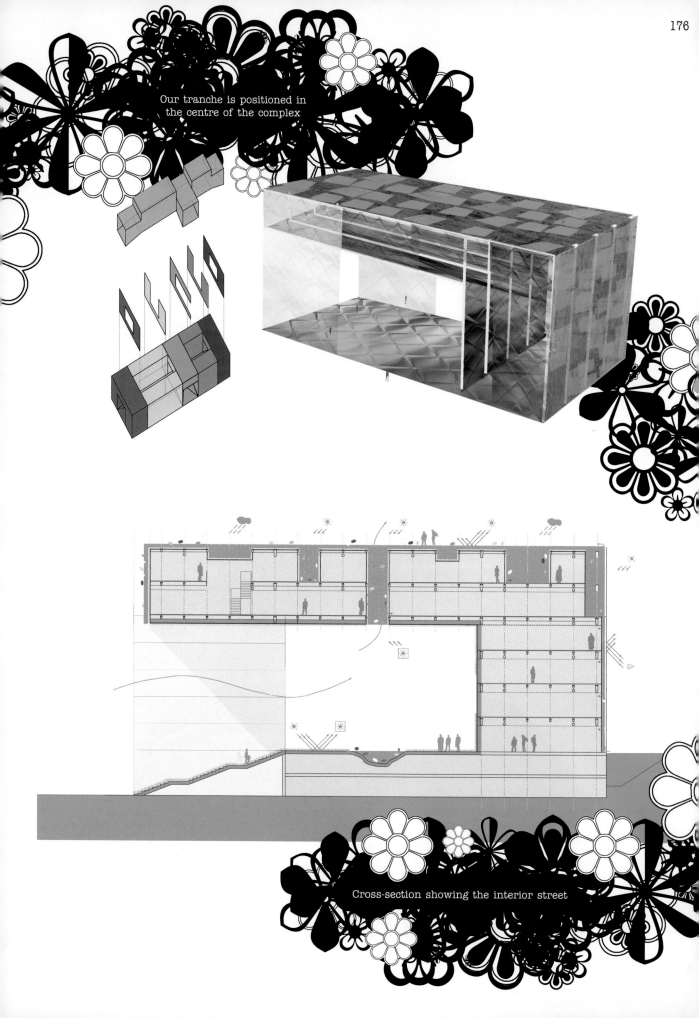

Our tranche is positioned in
the centre of the complex

Cross-section showing the interior street

View from the railway tracks (left to right: MVRDV, Pierre Gauthier, Manuelle Gautrand, Emmanuel Combarel/Dominique Marrec, Erick Van Egeraat)

The programme brings together housing and offices

View from the interior street

"LYON-CONFLUENCE"
Location: Lyon-Confluence quarter – Lyon – France
Competition: 2004 / Estimated handover: 2008
Client: ING and Atemi
Project team: Thomas Daragon (project manager),
Bertrand Colson, Yves Tougard, Maryline Gillois
Engineers: Khephren (structure), Van Santen (façade),
Alto (building fluids and ecological issues)
Surface area: 5,200 m²
Cost: €5 million, incl. tax

REDEVELOPMENT OF THE RECEPTION
AREA AND VIP SPACES AT CANAL+
(ISSY-LES-MOULINEAUX - FRANCE)

RESTRUCTURING
OF MAISON DE RADIO FRANCE
(PARIS)

2005

Anna
Szczeklik

Analia
Garcia Ramirez

Frédéric
Caudoux

ADMINISTRATIVE UNIT and Office building

Vincent
Sengel

Mieko
Levy Kobayashi

A thick grey and yellow ribbon ripples over the site, fluttering up and down, offering up spaces that form wide doors and crossings that open out onto the area housing the new administrative unit of the City Council.

Anna
Pujdak

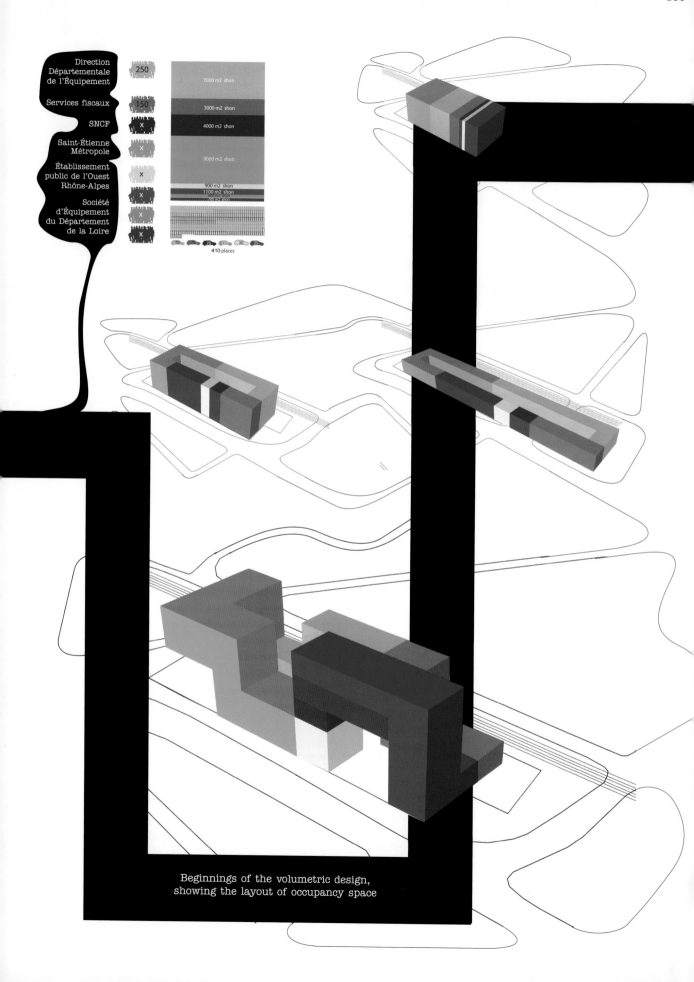

Direction
Départementale
de l'Équipement

Services fiscaux

SNCF

Saint-Étienne
Métropole

Établissement
public de l'Ouest
Rhône-Alpes

Société
d'Équipement
du Département
de la Loire

250

150

X
X
X
X
X

7000 m2 shon
3000 m2 shon
4000 m2 shon
9000 m2 shon
900 m2 shon
1100 m2 shon

410 places

Beginnings of the volumetric design,
showing the layout of occupancy space

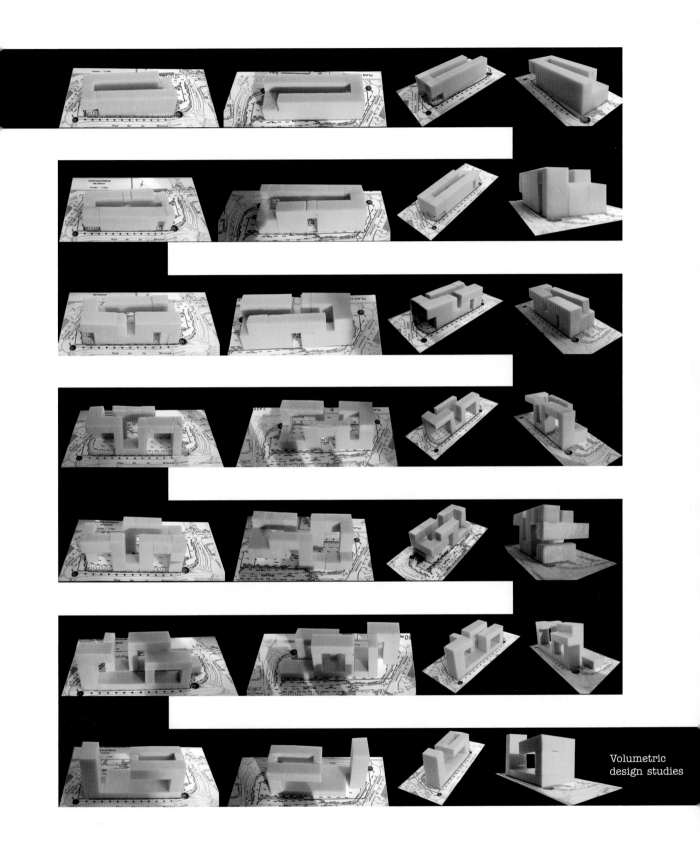

Volumetric
design studies

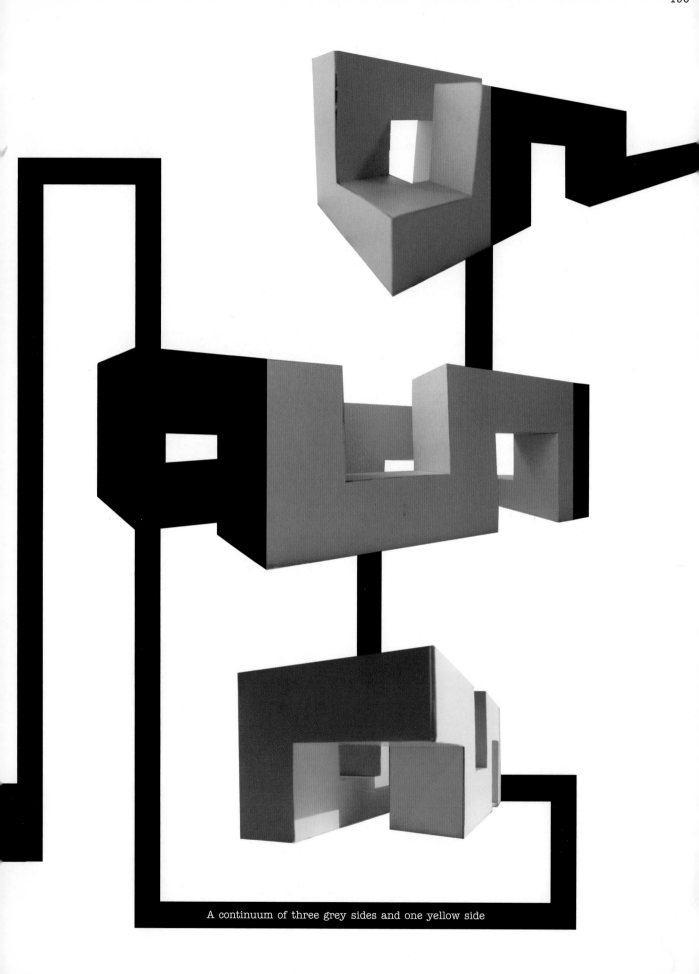

A continuum of three grey sides and one yellow side

South facade

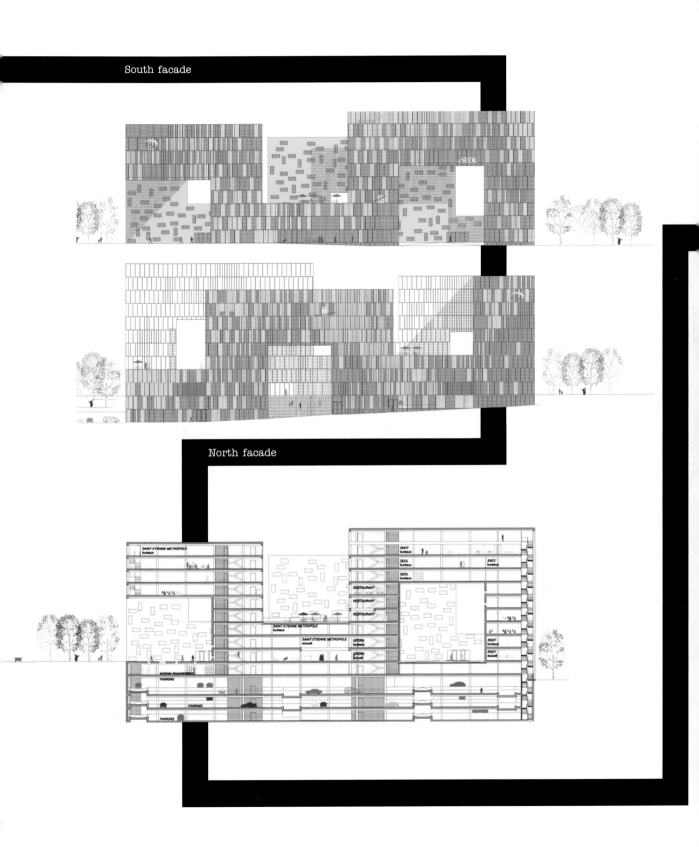

North facade

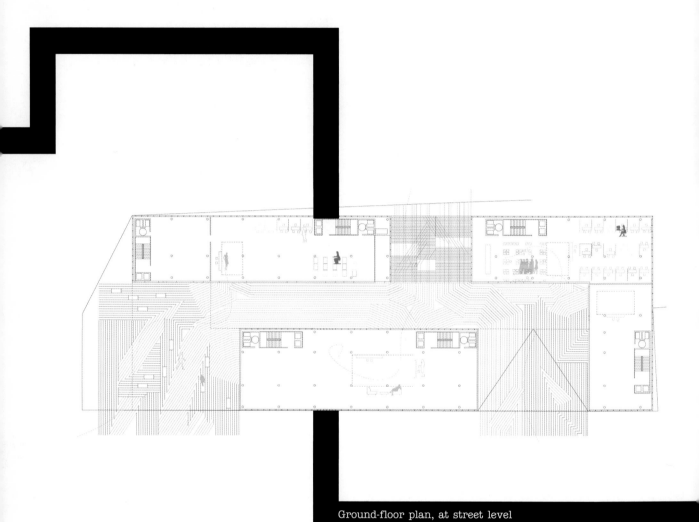

Ground-floor plan, at street level

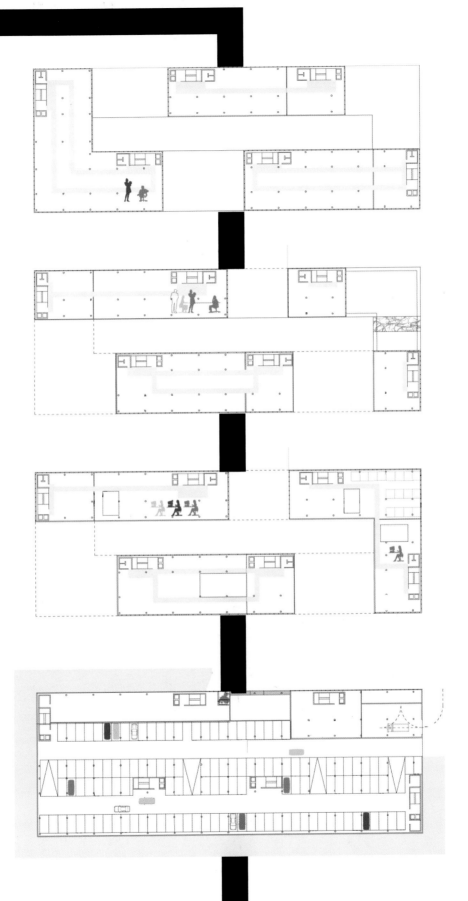

Main entrance of the administrative unit

ADMINISTRATIVE UNIT
Location: Grüner plot – Châteaucreux quarter
Saint-Etienne
Competition: 2005
Estimated handover: 2006 (phase 1), 2007 (phase 2)
Client: Cogedim / JFP Participation
Project team: Miléna Wysoczynska (project manager),
Yves Tougard (project manager of the design phase)
Sandrine Puech, Anna Pujdak, Anna Szczeklik,
Hendrik van Boetzelaer, Guillaume de Morsier
Surface area: 27,000 m²
Cost: €30 million, incl. tax

Endrik
van Boetzelaer

Guillaume
de Morsier

Manuel
Savoy

HOTEL, SPA AND RESTAURANT
ON ILE SEGUIN
(BOULOGNE-BILLANCOURT - FRANCE)

LA PORTE D'ISSY OFFICE BUILDING
(ISSY-LES-MOULINEAUX - FRANCE)

NEW LAW COURTS
(ROUEN - FRANCE)

Presentation of the architectural practice

Born in 1961, Manuelle Gautrand qualified as an architect in 1985. After working on several joint projects, she set up her own practice in Lyon in 1991, which she transferred to Paris in 1994.

Forming part of the new generation of French architects who combine public and private commissions, Manuelle Gautrand has already designed numerous projects in France and has been singled out in the French and international press. She has taken part in several major presentations and events, including the international consultation in 2001 for the François Pinault Foundation of Contemporary Art, and the Venice Biennale in 2002 and 2004. She has exhibited her sustainable development design studies at ARCHILAB in Orléans (France), and presented her Paris Docks project at the De Singel gallery in Antwerp, Belgium. In 2005, she was invited to the Deutsches Architektur Museum in Frankfurt to present her design for the Citroën showroom on the Champs-Elyées. As an active participant in the debating forum for contemporary concerns, Manuelle Gautrand has gained increasing acclaim on the international stage.

2004
Winner of the international "MIPIM Architectural Review" Future Project Awards 2005 for the Citroën showroom in Paris.

2003
Construction prize awarded by the Association of construction journalists.

2002
Delarue prize (silver medal) awarded by the Paris architecture academy.

2000
Winner of the French 2000 *Architecture et Maîtrise d'ouvrage prize* (architecture and the workplace category) for the catering building at Nantes airport.

1999
Nominated for the international Dupont Benedictus Award for the toll plazas on the A16 motorway.

1994
1994 Nominated for the *Première Œuvre du Moniteur* prize for the Le Fellini cinema at Villefontaine.

1992
Award-winner of *Albums de la Jeune Architecture.*

Manuelle Gautrand lectured at the Ecole Spéciale d'Architecture between 1999 and 2000 and at the Paris-Val-de-Seine school of architecture between 2000 and 2003. She currently teaches in architectural workshops held throughout Europe, notably in Karlsruhe, Madrid, Oslo, Riga, Vienna and Wroclaw. She also holds consulting positions, such as with the education authority in Grenoble since 1993, and the MIQCP since 1998 (Mission interministérielle pour la qualité des constructions publiques – French governmental body dedicated to overseeing the design quality of public buildings).
In 2005, Manuelle Gautrand was elected as a statutory member of the Paris architecture academy.

Thomas Daragon

Anne Feldmann

Gaëlle Le Borgne

Marc Blaising

Manuelle Gautrand

Shirin Raissi
Bertrand Colson

Marie Duval

Yves Tougard

Vincent Sengel

Frédéric Caudoux

Anna Szczeklik
Analia Garcia-Ramirez

Sandrine Puech

Frédéric Arnoult
Miléna Wysoczynska
Mathilde Tournyol du Clos
Marc Rihouey
Fanny Orihuela

Anna Pujdak

Manuel Savoy
Mieko Levy-Kobayashi

CURRENT DESIGNS AND PROJECTS

MAJOR BUILT WORHZES AND AWARDS

TEACHING POSTS/ CONSULTING WORK

Handover date

2008
Office building, Lyon Confluence quarter, Lyon

2007
Conversion of the Gaîté-Lyrique theatre into a centre dedicated to contemporary music and interactive arts, Paris
Extension-restructuring of the Lille Modern Art Museum, Villeneuve d'Ascq
Centre dedicated to the creation and staging of art performances, Rambouillet
Construction of an administrative unit, Châteaucreux quarter, Saint-Étienne

2006
Hélianthe residential complex comprising thirty-five apartments, Boulogne-Billancourt
Citroën showroom on the Avenue des Champs-Élysées, Paris
Solaris residential complex comprising 104 ecological apartments and a socio-cultural centre, Rennes

Handover date

2003 : international "MIPIM
Hydro Building System Review" Future Project
Batimat International Co for the Citroën
Fair, Paris   Paris.
Hospital laundry unit, L

2002   prize awarded
Two metro stations for tion of construction
Rennes

2001
La Coupole cultural cent (silver medal) awarded
comprising a theatre an rchitecture academy.
complex, Saint-Louis

1999   French 2000
Supply-chain warehouse et Maîtrise d'ouvrage
port de Gennevilliers   ture and the workplace
University institute of p he catering building
education dedicated to ir ort.
technology and logistics,

1998   the international
Nord-Pas-de-Calais natio ictus Award for the toll
centre, Béthune   A16 motorway.
Airport catering building
Toll plazas, A16 motorw
             ted for the Première
1997   niteur prize for the
Laurent-Mourguet schoo ma at Villefontaine.
Stopping point along the
Fontaine-sur-Saône
             of Albums de la Jeune
1996
Restructuring a two-scre
Saint-Priest
Restructuring the admir
unit of the Georges Pom
Paris
University institute of p
education, Annecy-le-Vieu
Airport warehouse, Nan

1995
Restructuring-extension
of a university building
to information technolog
Villeurbanne

1994
Le Fellini four-screen ci
Villefontaine

1993
Footbridge, Lyon

1992
Back-up IT centre for Re
Véhicules Industriels, Vé

Manuelle Gautrand lectured at the Ecole Spéciale d'Architecture between 1999 and 2000 and at the Paris-Val-de-Seine school of architecture between 2000 and 2003. She currently teaches in architectural workshops held throughout Europe, notably in Karlsruhe, Madrid, Oslo, Riga, Vienna and Wroclaw. She also holds consulting positions, such as with the education authority in Grenoble since 1993, and the MIQCP since 1998 (Mission interministérielle pour la qualité des constructions publiques – French governmental body dedicated to overseeing the design quality of public buildings).
In 2005, Manuelle Gautrand was elected as a statutory member of the Paris architecture academy.

CURRENT DESIGNS
AND PROJECTS

MAJOR BUILT WORKS

MAIN COMPETITIONS,
CONSULTATIONS
AND FEASIBILITY DESIGNS

Handover date

2008
Office building, Lyon Confluence
quarter, Lyon

2007
Conversion of the Gaîté-Lyrique
theatre into a centre dedicated to
contemporary music and interactive
arts, Paris
Extension-restructuring of the Lille
Modern Art Museum, Villeneuve
d'Ascq
Centre dedicated to the creation
and staging of art performances,
Rambouillet
Construction of an administrative
unit, Châteaucreux quarter,
Saint-Étienne

2006
Hélianthe residential complex
comprising thirty-five apartments,
Boulogne-Billancourt
Citroën showroom on the Avenue
des Champs-Élysées, Paris
Solaris residential complex comprising
104 ecological apartments and
a socio-cultural centre, Rennes

Handover date

2003
Hydro Building System Stand,
Batimat International Construction
Fair, Paris
Hospital laundry unit, Le Havre

2002
Two metro stations for the Val line,
Rennes

2001
La Coupole cultural centre
comprising a theatre and cinema
complex, Saint-Louis

1999
Supply-chain warehouse,
port de Gennevilliers
University institute of professional
education dedicated to information
technology and logistics, Lieusaint

1998
Nord-Pas-de-Calais national drama
centre, Béthune
Airport catering building, Nantes
Toll plazas, A16 motorway

1997
Laurent-Mourguet school, Écully
Stopping point along the Saône river,
Fontaine-sur-Saône

1996
Restructuring a two-screen cinema,
Saint-Priest
Restructuring the administrative
unit of the Georges Pompidou Centre,
Paris
University institute of professional
education, Annecy-le-Vieux
Airport warehouse, Nantes

1995
Restructuring-extension
of a university building dedicated
to information technology,
Villeurbanne

1994
Le Fellini four-screen cinema,
Villefontaine

1993
Footbridge, Lyon

1992
Back-up IT centre for Renault
Véhicules Industriels, Vénissieux

2005
Restructuring Maison
de Radio-France, Paris
Redeveloping visitor and VIP
spaces at Canal+ television studios,
Issy-les-Moulineaux
Complex of apartments, shops and
offices, Euralille II, Lille
La Porte d'Issy office building,
Issy-les-Moulineaux
New law courts, Rouen
Hotel, l'Ile Seguin, Boulogne-Billancourt
Complex of collective and individual
residential units, Blagnac

2004
Office building for the PSA
research unit, Vélizy
Paris Docks leisure area, Paris
"Enveloping façade", l'Ile Seguin,
Boulogne-Billancourt
Office building, Orléans
Casino Group headquarters,
Saint-Étienne
La Place Nautique residential complex,
Lyon-Confluence quarter, Lyon
Reconstruction of the Avaricum
district – apartments, hotel, shops,
Bourges

2003
"Le Bois Habité" – ecological
apartments, Lille
Port storage warehouse,
Saint-Nazaire port
Daugava riverside development, Riga
(Latvia)
Development of a tertiary area,
Greater Paris region

2002
Contemporary music centre, Nancy
Image Pavilion, designed for the 2004
International Exhibition, Dugny
Redevelopment of Place
Charles-de-Gaulle, Rennes

2001
Residential complex comprising
260 apartments, Montévrain
Conversion of the "Halles aux
Farines" (flour exchange building)
into a social sciences university,
Paris
François Pinault Foundation
of Contemporary Art, l'Ile Seguin,
Boulogne-Billancourt

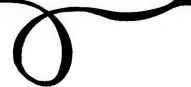

Outside France

2004
"Post-Modernism Revisited",
Citroën project, Deutsches Architektur
Museum (DAM), Frankfurt, Germany
"Métamorph", ninth international
architecture exhibition of the Venice
Biennale, Italy

2002
"Hybrid landscapes: apartments
in Rennes", Valence school of
architecture, Spain
"Cultural platform in Paris",
De Singel international arts centre,
Antwerp, Belgium
"Next", eighth international
architecture exhibition of the Venice
Biennale, Italy
"Hybrid landscapes: apartments
in Rennes", Maison de France, Berlin,
Germany

2001
"Hybrid landscapes: apartments
in Rennes", Alliance Française,
Rotterdam, the Netherlands
"Rushes: Airport building in Nantes",
ASA salon, Bangkok, Thailand

2000
"U2000: Institut universitaire
de Lieusaint", Villa Finaly, Florence,
Italy

1999
"Rushes: Airport building in Nantes",
French Institute, Madrid, Spain / Imzu
gallery, Hakata, Japan

1998
"New wave", Kaikan gallery,
Kagoshima, Japan / Taisei gallery,
Tokyo, Japan

1995
"Public spaces in Lyon", Brussels
museum of fine arts, Belgium

In France

2004
"La nouvelle Gaîté Lyrique",
Pavillon de l'Arsenal, Paris
"Centre de communication Citroën",
Pavillon de l'Arsenal, Paris

2003
"Inaccoutumance", La Galerie
d'Architecture, Paris
"Mini-Maousse" Bulle Bulle Casa,
Jardin du Luxembourg, Paris
"A comme Architecture", Galerie
Duchamps, Yvetot
"Extension du musée d'Art moderne
de Lille", Villeneuve d'Ascq modern
art museum
"Carrosseries…: Projet Citroën",
C.A.U.E. 92, Sceaux

2002
"Territoires partagés: Entrepôt A12
à Gennevilliers", Pavillon de l'Arsenal,
Paris
"L'architecture des stations
de métro", Centre d'information
sur l'urbanisme, Rennes
"Deux projets culturels",
ARCHILAB-FRAC Centre, Orléans
"Architecture et Pédagogie",
La Sorbonne, Paris

2001
"Les maisons du bonheur",
Institut français d'architecture, Paris
"Habiter aujourd'hui",
ARCHILAB-FRAC Centre, Orléans
"Temps, matière, architecture",
Maison de l'architecture de l'Isère,
Grenoble

1999
"Rushes: Bâtiment aéroportuaire
de Nantes", Galerie Paillard, Marseille
"Objets d'architectes", Galerie IDM,
Nantes

1997
"Actualité architecturale",
Institut français d'architecture, Paris

1993
"Maquettes à Troyes",
Institut français d'architecture, Paris

1992
"Albums Jeune Architecture",
Maison de l'architecture, Paris

MAIN SYMPOSIA, LECTURES AND WORKSHOPS

Outside France

2004
"Recent projects", Oslo school of architecture, Norway
"Architecture in France", REFE salon, Warsaw, Poland

2003
Workshop and lecture, Riga School of architecture, Latvia

2002
Workshop, Technical University of Vienna, Austria
"Plaisirs d'architecture", Fondation de l'Architecture, Luxembourg
"European seminar on young architects", Antwerp congress hall, Belgium
"Hybrid landscapes: apartments in Rennes", Maison de France, Berlin, Germany
"Zwischen Alltag und Vision", Karlsruhe University, Germany

2001
Lecture and workshop, International Symposium of Architecture, Monterey, Mexico

2000
"Le Sud", Technical University of Vienna, Austria

1999
"Recent projects", French Institute, Madrid, Spain

In France

2004
"Développement commercial et architecture innovante", MAPIC salon, Cannes
"Le patrimoine de demain", Maison de l'architecture, Paris
"Le patrimoine est-il recyclable", Cultural Affairs Department, City of Paris
"Projets en cours", Georges Pompidou Centre, Paris

2003
"La maîtrise d'ouvrage privée", École Spéciale d'Architecture, Paris
"Plaisir d'Architecture", Montpellier school of architecture
"Panorama des projets de l'agence", Lille school of architecture

2002
"Musées, marketing, communication", Chartres
"L'Architecture", Université Populaire, Le Lieu Unique, Nantes
"Architecture et espaces publics", Centre d'information et d'urbanisme, Rennes
"Economie de la terre", ARCHILAB - Frac Centre, Orléans
"Parti architectural et énergie", EDF Forum – Sustainable Development, Paris
"Maîtrise d'œuvre et accès à la commande", round table discussion organized by Moniteur des Travaux Publics, Paris
"Panorama des projets de l'agence", Strasbourg and Rennes schools of architecture

2001
"Panorama des projets de l'agence", Marseille school of architecture

2000
"La matière", arc-en-rêve architectural centre, Bordeaux
"Les femmes dans l'architecture", Institut français d'architecture, Paris
"Young French architects", Institut français d'architecture, Paris
"Panorama des projets de l'agence", École Spéciale d'Architecture, Paris

1999
"L'aménagement du campus universitaire de Grenoble", French Ministry of National Education, Paris

1998
"Panorama des projets de l'agence", Paris-la-Seine school of architecture

1997
"Panorama des projets de l'agence", Nantes, Grenoble and Bordeaux schools of architecture

Monographs

DD, Design Document Series-06, Manuelle Gautrand, DAMDI Co., Seoul, February 2004.

La Coupole à Saint-Louis, Manuelle Gautrand, Ante Prima / Diagonale, Rome, 2003.

Collective works

Flush! Modern Toilet Design, Ingrid Wenz-Gahler, Birkhäuser, Basel, Boston, Berlin, 2005. Architecture Highlights,

Post-Modernism revisited, international exhibition catalogue, Deutsches Architektur Museum Frankfurt, Junius Verlag, Hamburg, 2004.

Architecture Highlights, Shanglin A&C Ltd., Bejing, China, 2004.

Paris: Architecture & Design, teNeues, Kempen, 2004.

Architecture Now, vol. III, Philip Jodidio, Taschen, Köln, 2004.

Métropoles en Europe, Éditions du Moniteur, Paris, 2004.

1000 architects, listing to the world's leading architects, the Images Publishing group, Victoria, Australia, 2004.

Metamorph, ninth international architecture exhibition of the Venice Biennale, Marsilio Editore, Venice, 2004.

ARCHILAB'S Earth Buildings, Radical Experiments in Land Architecture, Marie-Ange Brayer & Béatrice Simonot, Thames and Hudson, London, 2003.

Économie de la terre: plateforme culturelle, ARCHILAB 2002, HYX, Orléans, 2002.

Créateurs Création en France, La scène contemporaine, supervised by Nathalie Chapuis, Éditions Autrement, Paris, 2002.

Contextes, catalogue for the French Pavilion, eighth international architecture exhibition of the Venice Biennale, HYX, Orléans, 2002.

Carchitecture: when the car and the city collide, Jonathan Bell, Birkhäuser, Basel, Boston, Berlin, 2002.

Construire avec les aciers, Éditions du Moniteur, Paris, 2002.

Innovations durables. Une autre architecture française / Appropriate Sustainabilities. New Ways in French Architecture, supervised by Marc Emery, Ante Prima / Birkhäuser, Paris, Basel, Boston, Berlin, 2002.

Temps dense 2, supervised by Lionel Blaisse and François Gaillard, Édition de l'Imprimeur, Besançon, 2001.

"Logements HQE", ARCHILAB 2001, HYX, Orléans, 2001.

Sans doute? Cent architectes parlent doctrine, Les Cahiers de la recherche architecturale et urbaine, n° 5/6, Éditions du Patrimoine, Paris, 2000.

40 architects under 40 years, Jessica Cargill Thompson, Taschen, Köln, 2000.

Young French Architects / Jeunes Architectes Français, Corinne Jaquand-Goddefroy, Claus Kapplinger, Birkhäuser, Basel, Boston, Berlin, 1999.

Manuelle Gautrand's work has featured in a large number of press articles, including:

• in French architectural journals, such as *Architecture Créé, Archistorm, Moniteur AMC, Techniques et Architecture;*

• in international reviews, such as: *Bauwelt, Details* (Germany), *Abstract* (Belgium), *AV Proyectos, Pasajes de Arquitectura* (Spain), *Architectural Records* (The United States), *Abitare, Cluster, l'Arca, Ottagono* (Italy), *A+U, Casa Brutus, Chinkenchiku* (Japan), *Archis, De Architect* (The Netherlands), *Monitor Unlimited* (Russia), and *Idea* (Switzerland)

• in newspapers and magazines, including *Beaux-Arts Magazine, Citizen K, L'Express, Le Monde, Le Figaro, Le Journal des Arts, Les Échos, Télérama,* (France), *El Pais* (Spain) and *Die Zeit* (Germany)